YORKSHIRE DALES TRAVEL GUIDE 2026

Discover England's Green Heart – Rolling Hills, Stone Villages, Local Charm and Timeless Adventures

By

JANET D. BOSWELL

DISCLAIMER

This Yorkshire Dales Travel Guide 2025-2026 is intended for general informational and planning purposes only. While every effort has been made to ensure the accuracy and reliability of the content, details such as prices, opening hours, locations, services, and local regulations are subject to change without notice. Travelers are responsible for verifying current information before making reservations, visiting attractions, or engaging in activities.

The guide does not provide medical, legal, or safety advice specific to individual circumstances. Readers should consult relevant professionals, official authorities, or trusted local sources for guidance on health, safety, visas, insurance, and other specialized needs. The authors and publishers are not liable for any loss, injury, or inconvenience that may occur as a result of using this guide.

Travelers should exercise personal judgment, follow local laws and customs, and prioritize safety at all times. The information provided is intended to enhance the travel experience, but it cannot guarantee outcomes, prevent accidents, or address all potential risks. Use this guide as a practical reference, and combine it with up-to-date resources and your own careful planning for a safe and enjoyable visit to Istanbul.

TABLE OF CONTENT

1. Introduction to the Yorkshire Dales — 5
   1.1 Why Visit the Yorkshire Dales? — 6
   1.2 How to Use This Guide — 7
   1.3 History, Culture & Traditions of the Dales — 8

2. Planning Your Trip — 13
   2.1 Best Time to Visit & Weather by Season — 13
   2.2 Getting There & Around (Car, Train, Bus & Walking) — 16
   2.3 Travel Costs, Passes & Budgeting Tips — 20
   2.4 Sustainable & Responsible Travel — 23

3. Exploring the Dales: Towns & Villages — 27
   3.1 Grassington, Hawes & Reeth — 27
   3.3 Hidden Gems: Smaller Villages Worth a Stop — 31

4. Natural Wonders & Top Attractions of the Dales — 38
   4.1 Famous Landscapes: Malham Cove, Gordale Scar & Ingleborough — 38
   4.2 Waterfalls: Aysgarth Falls, Hardraw Force & Hidden Streams — 44
   4.3 Geological Marvels: Ribblehead Viaduct, White Scar Cave & Limestone Pavements — 48
   4.4 Valleys & Countryside Charm: Swaledale, Wensleydale & Wharfedale — 51
   4.5 Wildlife & Nature Reserves — 56

5. Outdoor Adventures — 60
   5.1 Walking & Hiking Trails for All Levels — 60
   5.2 Cycling & Mountain Biking Routes — 65
   5.3 Caving, Climbing & Adventure Sports — 69

6. Cultural Experiences & Heritage — 75
   6.1 Castles, Abbeys & Historic Sites — 75
   6.2 Museums & Folk Traditions — 77
   6.3 Local Festivals, Events & Fairs — 80

7. Food & Drink of the Dales — 84
   7.1 Traditional Yorkshire Cuisine — 84
   7.2 Local Pubs, Tea Rooms & Farm Shops — 86
   7.3 Food Experiences & Farmers' Markets — 88
   7.3 Food Experiences & Farmers' Markets — 89

8. Where to Stay in the Yorkshire Dales — 91
   8.1 Cozy Cottages, B&Bs & Inns — 91
   8.2 Family-Friendly Stays & Camping — 93
   8.3 Luxury Retreats & Unique Accommodations — 94

9. Suggested Itineraries — **98**
    9.1 2-Day Highlights of the Dales — 98
    9.2 4–5 Day Journey Through Villages & Landscapes — 100
    9.3 A Full Week in the Dales: History, Hiking & Hidden Gems — 103

10. Practical Travel Tips & Resources — **107**
    10.1 Safety, Weather & Outdoor Preparedness — 107
    10.2 Communication & Connectivity in Rural Areas — 109
    10.3 Final Thoughts & Inspiring Itineraries — 111

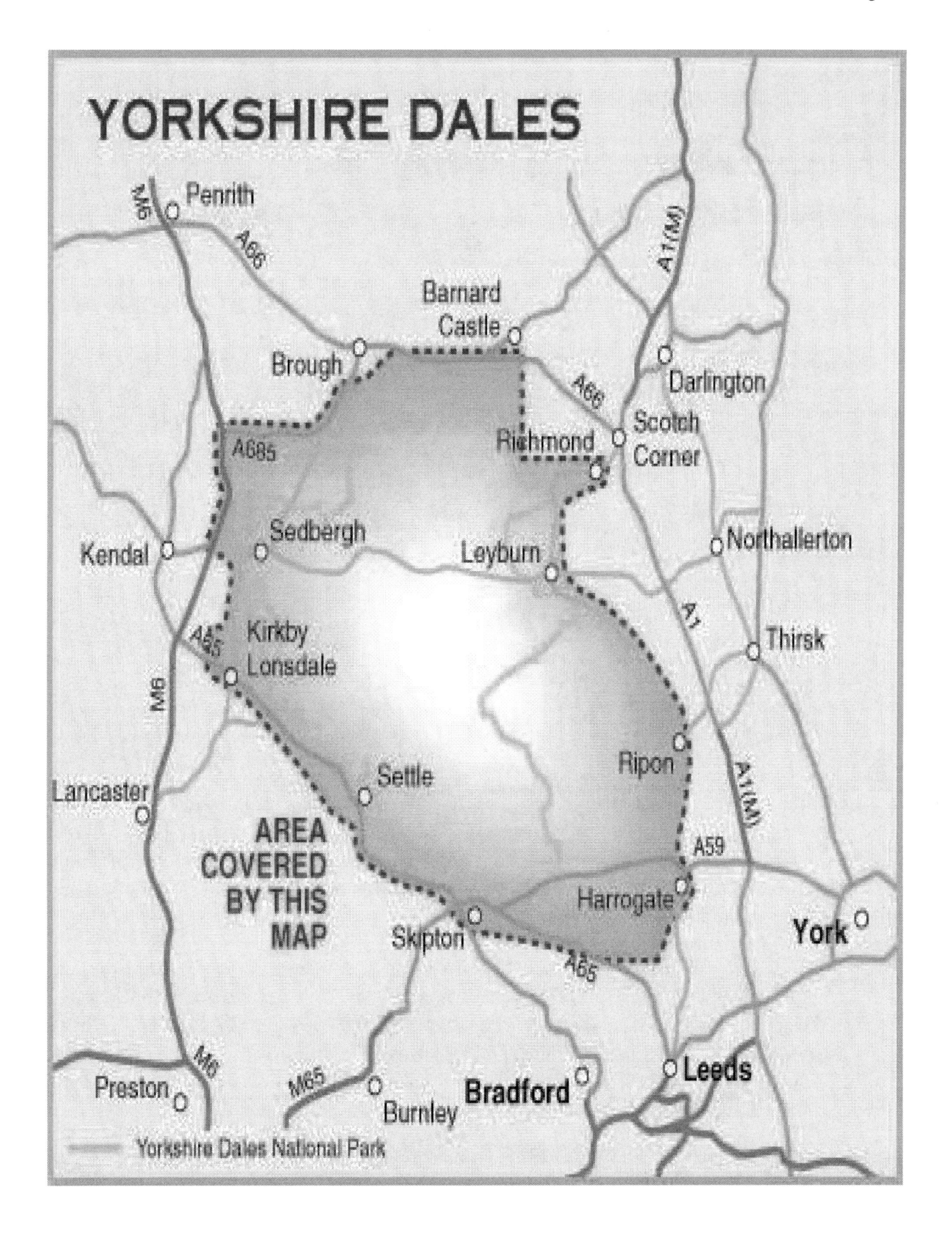

YORKSHIRE DALES

AREA COVERED BY THIS MAP

— Yorkshire Dales National Park

1. Introduction to the Yorkshire Dales

The Yorkshire Dales are a part of England that feels timeless. Here, rolling green valleys stretch out between rugged hills, rivers sparkle in the sun, and stone-built villages welcome visitors with warmth and charm. It's a place where nature, history, and tradition come together, offering the perfect escape for anyone who loves the outdoors, good food, and a slower pace of life.

The Dales cover a wide area across North Yorkshire and parts of Cumbria and Lancashire. Each valley, or "dale," has its own character—**Wensleydale** with its cheese and waterfalls, **Swaledale** with its wild beauty and curlews calling across the hills, **Wharfedale** with handsome villages, and **Ribblesdale**, home to the famous Yorkshire Three Peaks. What ties them together is the mixture of dramatic landscapes and small, welcoming communities that make you feel at home straight away.

1.1 Why Visit the Yorkshire Dales?

There are many reasons people fall in love with the Yorkshire Dales, and each visit can be different.

For the landscapes. The Dales are full of natural wonders—**Malham Cove's** towering limestone cliffs, the dramatic gorge of **Gordale Scar**, the thunder of **Aysgarth Falls**, and the elegance of **Hardraw Force**. You'll find broad moors, peaceful riversides, rolling meadows, and caves like **White Scar**, all waiting to be explored. Whether you want gentle valley strolls or challenging hill climbs, the scenery is unforgettable.

For the villages and towns. Life here is centered around traditional market towns and stone-built villages. **Hawes, Grassington, Skipton, Settle, Reeth,** and **Richmond** each have their own charm, with cobbled squares, weekly markets, independent shops, and inns that feel like part of the community. These aren't just tourist stops—they're working places where history and modern life meet.

For the history and heritage. The Dales are steeped in the past. You can explore the ruins of **Bolton Abbey**, walk under the arches of the **Ribblehead Viaduct**, or follow trails once used by monks, miners, and drovers. The dry-stone walls and field barns you see in the meadows aren't decoration—they're part of centuries of farming tradition.

For food and hospitality. This is Yorkshire, so you can expect hearty, honest food. Taste **Wensleydale cheese** at its source, enjoy a pint of locally brewed ale in a centuries-old pub, or sit down to tea and scones in a cozy tearoom. Don't be surprised if a stranger strikes up a conversation—the friendliness here is genuine.

For the seasons. Each time of year has its charm. Spring brings lambs and wildflowers, summer offers long days on the hills, autumn glows with rich colors, and winter feels magical with frosty mornings and starry skies. Thanks to its **Dark Sky Reserve** status, the Dales are one of the best places in England to see the night sky.

For peace and simplicity. Perhaps the best reason to visit is how the Dales make you feel. There's space here—to breathe, to walk, to notice small details like birdsong or the sound of a river. It's an escape from fast-paced life, but it doesn't feel cut off. You can still find comfort, good food, and welcoming people at the end of the day.

In short, the Yorkshire Dales offer something for everyone—whether you're chasing adventure, looking for history, or simply wanting to relax in beautiful surroundings. It's the kind of place that leaves you refreshed, inspired, and already planning your return.

1.2 How to Use This Guide

This guide is designed to be your companion before, during, and even after your trip to the Yorkshire Dales. Think of it as both an inspiration and a practical handbook. If you're planning your first visit, you'll find clear explanations of what makes the Dales special, along with tips to help you organize your journey smoothly. If you've been before, this book will help you dig deeper—showing you hidden corners, less-traveled paths, and local secrets.

Each chapter has a specific purpose. Early sections introduce you to the Dales' history, culture, and natural beauty, giving you a sense of place. The planning chapters help with practical details such as when to go, how to get around, and where to stay. Later chapters dive into must-see attractions, hikes, villages, and seasonal experiences so you can make the most of your time.

You don't have to read the book in order. If you're short on time, jump straight to the attractions or hiking sections. If you're in the mood for inspiration, browse the photography and scenic highlights. Travelers who want to learn more about the people and traditions of the Dales can go to the cultural and historical insights chapter.

In short, this guide is flexible. Use it as a reference, a source of ideas, or a step-by-step planner. Whether you're here for a weekend escape or a longer adventure, you'll find everything you need to enjoy the Yorkshire Dales to the fullest.

1.3 History, Culture & Traditions of the Dales

The Yorkshire Dales is more than just rolling hills, stone walls, and sheep-dotted meadows—it is a living landscape, deeply shaped by its history and the traditions of the people who have called it home for thousands of years. To truly appreciate the valleys, villages, and walking paths of the Dales, you have to look beyond the scenery and understand the layers of human life that have unfolded here. From prehistoric settlers and Viking farmers to medieval monasteries and modern-day walkers, the Dales has always been a meeting ground of nature, culture, and community.

This chapter takes you through that story: the roots of the Dales' history, its unique rural culture, the traditions that still thrive, and the spirit of resilience that defines the region today.

Ancient Roots: Prehistoric and Roman Influences

Human activity in the Yorkshire Dales stretches back thousands of years. Archaeologists have uncovered evidence of prehistoric communities who farmed and hunted in these valleys as far back as the Neolithic period (around 4000–2500 BC). Standing stones, stone circles, and burial mounds can still be found in parts of the Dales, silent witnesses to the early communities who lived here.

One of the most striking prehistoric landmarks is the stone circle at **Yockenthwaite**, thought to be a Bronze Age ritual site. Places like this remind us that the Dales have always been a place where humans felt a connection to the land, not only for survival but also for spiritual meaning.

Later, the Romans arrived in Britain (AD 43–410) and left their mark on the Dales as well. Although this rugged upland was not the center of Roman activity, evidence of Roman roads and forts survives. Roman soldiers built key routes through the Pennines, linking fortresses like **Bainbridge (Virosidum)** with other parts of northern England. These roads helped shape later settlement patterns and even influenced modern walking paths.

Viking and Norse Heritage

Perhaps one of the strongest cultural imprints on the Yorkshire Dales comes from the Vikings. After arriving in the 9th century, Norse settlers established farms, cleared valleys, and gave names to many of the places we still use today. The word "dale" itself comes from the Old Norse "dalr," meaning valley.

Look at a map of the Dales and you'll spot countless Viking place names:

- Words ending in **-thwaite** (like Satterthwaite), meaning clearing.
- **-beck**, meaning stream.
- **-gill**, meaning narrow valley.

These names are not just linguistic relics—they reflect the Viking way of life as farmers and herders, who made their living in this rugged land. The Norse influence is still deeply embedded in the Yorkshire dialect and in local farming traditions that have survived through the centuries.

Monastic Life and Medieval Villages

By the Middle Ages, the Dales had become home to powerful monasteries that transformed both the economy and the landscape. The **Cistercian monks**, in particular, established great abbeys such as **Fountains Abbey** (a UNESCO World Heritage Site today), **Bolton Priory**, and **Jervaulx Abbey**.

The monks were not only spiritual leaders but also pioneering farmers and land managers. They introduced large-scale sheep farming, clearing forests and enclosing land. Wool produced in the Dales became one of England's most valuable exports, linking these quiet valleys to the global economy of the medieval world.

The ruins of these monasteries still stand as hauntingly beautiful reminders of that era. Walk through the arches of Bolton Priory or the cloisters of Fountains Abbey, and you can almost hear the echo of chanting monks mixed with the bleating of sheep.

Medieval villages also flourished during this time. Settlements like Grassington and Reeth grew as centers of trade, markets, and farming. Stone cottages, churches, and market squares from this period still form the heart of many Dales communities.

Industry, Mining & The Making of the Modern Dales

While farming and sheep remained central to life in the Dales, the Industrial Revolution brought new changes. From the 17th to the 19th centuries, lead mining became a dominant industry in parts of the Dales, especially in Swaledale and Arkengarthdale.

Entire communities worked the mines, and remnants of old smelting mills, chimneys, and spoil heaps can still be found scattered across the moorlands.

Though mining brought jobs and money, it also reshaped the land—leaving scars on the hillsides and creating harsh conditions for workers. By the late 19th century, as the industry declined, many families left in search of better opportunities elsewhere. Yet, the traces of that mining heritage remain an important part of the cultural memory of the Dales.

The coming of the railways in the 19th century also changed the region. The most famous is the **Settle–Carlisle Railway**, which cuts a dramatic line through the Dales with its stone viaducts and tunnels. This railway not only provided vital transport for goods and people but also opened the Dales to tourism. For the first time, visitors from industrial cities like Leeds and Manchester could escape to the countryside for fresh air and relaxation.

Farming, Sheep, and the Rural Way of Life

If there is one symbol of the Yorkshire Dales, it is the sheep. For centuries, sheep farming has been the backbone of the local economy and the defining feature of its culture. The iconic dry-stone walls crisscrossing the hillsides were built to divide pastures and protect flocks. The distinctive stone barns scattered across fields—known as "laithes"—were used to shelter sheep and store hay.

Different breeds of sheep, such as the Swaledale and Wensleydale, are native to the region and have shaped its agricultural identity. Farmers here have long worked with the land in a sustainable way, passing down knowledge from one generation to the next.

Life on a Dales farm has never been easy. The weather can be harsh, the land difficult to manage, and the markets unpredictable. Yet farming families have preserved a strong sense of independence, community, and tradition. Today, many still gather at agricultural shows, where sheepdog trials, livestock competitions, and rural crafts celebrate the farming heritage.

Folklore, Legends & Storytelling

Like many rural regions, the Dales has its share of folklore and legends passed down through the generations. Stories of ghosts haunting old abbeys, mysterious creatures roaming the moors, and heroic local figures are part of the oral tradition that enriches the culture of the Dales.

One famous tale is that of **The Barguest**, a mythical black dog said to haunt lonely lanes and graveyards. Another is the legend of **Janet's Foss**, a waterfall near Malham named after a fairy queen said to dwell in its pool.

These stories reflect the deep connection people here have always had with the land, blending fear, wonder, and respect for the forces of nature. Even today, storytelling remains an important tradition, whether through local writers, folk music, or community events.

Dialect, Music, and Arts

The Yorkshire dialect is part of what makes the Dales feel so distinctive. Though it has evolved over time, echoes of Old Norse and Old English remain in the words and phrases still used by locals. The rhythm and sound of Dale's speech carry a warmth and authenticity that visitors quickly notice.

Music has also long been part of Dales culture. Folk songs often tell of farming life, mining struggles, or local legends. Traditional instruments like the fiddle or accordion accompany dances at community gatherings. Today, folk festivals and local choirs continue to keep this heritage alive.

In more recent years, the beauty of the Dales has inspired countless artists, writers, and photographers. From the paintings of J.M.W. Turning to the writings of James Herriot (the famous Yorkshire vet and author), the landscape continues to fuel creativity and storytelling that resonates far beyond Yorkshire.

Community, Traditions & Celebrations

Perhaps the most enduring aspect of Dales culture is its strong sense of community. Villages here are often small, but they are tightly knit, with traditions that bring people together. Agricultural shows, such as the **Kilnsey Show** or the **Reeth Show**, celebrate rural skills and livestock. Local pubs serve not just as places to eat and drink but as social centers where news, music, and laughter are shared.

Seasonal celebrations also play an important role. From Christmas carol singing in stone churches to May Day festivities and summer fairs, these traditions keep community life vibrant.

Hospitality is another hallmark of the Dales. Visitors often remark on the friendliness of the locals, who are proud of their heritage and eager to share it with newcomers. That welcoming spirit is as much a part of the Dales experience as the scenery itself.

The Yorkshire Identity Today

While the Yorkshire Dales has deep roots in history, it is not stuck in the past. Modern communities balance tradition with change. Farming remains vital, but tourism now plays a central role in the economy. Walkers, cyclists, and nature lovers from all over the world come to experience the landscapes, supporting local businesses from tearooms to B&Bs.

At the same time, conservation efforts ensure that the natural beauty and cultural heritage are protected for future generations. The designation of the Dales as a **National Park (1954)** has helped safeguard its character, while local initiatives keep traditions alive in a rapidly changing world.

To visit the Yorkshire Dales is to step into a living story—where ancient stone walls meet modern footpaths, where centuries-old traditions still shape daily life, and where the people's resilience is as enduring as the hills themselves.

2. Planning Your Trip

2.1 Best Time to Visit & Weather by Season

One of the first questions most travelers ask is, *"When is the best time to visit the Yorkshire Dales?"* The truth is, there isn't one simple answer. The Dales are a year-round destination, each season offering its own beauty, atmosphere, and unique experiences. Your choice will depend on what you want from your trip—long sunny hikes, cozy pub evenings by a roaring fire, quiet villages free from crowds, or dramatic landscapes wrapped in snow and mist.

To help you decide, let's break it down season by season:

Spring (March – May)

Spring is a season of renewal in the Dales. After the quiet and often harsh winter, the countryside comes alive with fresh greenery, blossoming wildflowers, and the playful energy of lambs in the meadows.

- **Weather**: Temperatures usually range between 7°C (45°F) in March and 15°C (59°F) in May. Rain is still common, but there are more dry, sunny spells as the season progresses. Days get noticeably longer, giving you more daylight for outdoor activities.
- **Highlights**:

- - **Wildflowers & Wildlife**: Daffodils in the woods, bluebells carpeting the valleys, and curlews calling across the moors.
  - **Lambing Season**: Farms and fields are full of young lambs—an iconic sight in the Dales.
  - **Easter Traditions**: Many villages host small fairs, craft markets, or church services that reflect the rural community spirit.
- **Best For**: Walkers who enjoy moderate temperatures, nature lovers, and photographers who want the best balance of light, greenery, and activity.

Tip: Pack a good pair of waterproof boots—trails can still be muddy after winter rains.

Summer (June – August)

Summer is the most popular time to visit the Yorkshire Dales, and for good reason. Long days, warmer temperatures, and vibrant festivals make it the peak season for walkers, families, and first-time visitors.

- **Weather**: Average temperatures range from 15°C (59°F) to 22°C (72°F). While this isn't "hot" by global standards, it's very pleasant for walking. Rain can still occur—this is England, after all—but you're likely to enjoy more stable conditions.
- **Highlights**:
  - **Walking & Hiking**: Famous routes like the Three Peaks Challenge, Malham Cove trails, and the waterfalls of Ingleton are at their most inviting.
  - **Festivals & Shows**: The summer calendar is full of agricultural shows, music festivals, and food fairs celebrating Dales culture.
  - **Outdoor Activities**: From cycling through quiet lanes to canoeing in rivers, summer is when everything is open and running.
- **Best For**: Hikers, families with children, festival lovers, and those who prefer lively village life.

Tip: This is the busiest season. If you prefer solitude, start your hikes early in the morning or venture to less-visited valleys like Swaledale.

Autumn (September – November)

Autumn brings a quieter, reflective beauty to the Dales. The crowds thin out, the landscapes turn shades of gold and red, and there's a crisp freshness in the air.

- **Weather**: Early autumn is mild, with September still offering temperatures around 14°C (57°F). By November, it drops to 6–8°C (43–46°F). Rain increases, and misty mornings become common.
- **Highlights**:
    - **Changing Landscapes**: Heather blooms purple across the moors in late August and September, followed by colorful woodlands in October.
    - **Food & Drink**: Autumn is harvest season, and local pubs often feature hearty, seasonal dishes—perfect after a long walk.
    - **Peaceful Walks**: Trails are quieter, allowing you to enjoy places like Bolton Abbey or Aysgarth Falls without summer crowds.
- **Best For**: Couples looking for romance, photographers, and those who enjoy cozy evenings after bracing outdoor walks.

Tip: Days get shorter quickly—plan hikes to finish before nightfall. Always carry a torch (flashlight) if you're out late.

Winter (December – February)

Winter is the most challenging season in the Dales but also one of the most magical. Snow-dusted hills, frozen waterfalls, and smoke rising from village chimneys create a postcard-perfect atmosphere.

- **Weather**: Average temperatures range between 2–6°C (35–43°F), but it can drop below freezing, especially in higher areas. Snow and ice are possible, particularly on the hills, while valleys may experience heavy frost and rain.
- **Highlights**:
    - **Peace & Solitude**: Few visitors come in winter, so you'll have trails and villages almost to yourself.
    - **Snowy Scenery**: Malham Cove and Pen-y-ghent covered in snow are unforgettable sights.
    - **Cozy Evenings**: Pubs with roaring fires, mulled drinks, and warm Yorkshire puddings make winter trips special.
- **Best For**: Adventurers who enjoy challenging hikes, romantic winter getaways, and travelers seeking solitude.

Tip: Be prepared. Some roads may be icy, smaller guesthouses might close, and public transport can be limited. Always check weather forecasts and trail conditions before setting out.

So, When Should You Go?

- **For Hiking**: Late spring (May–June) and early autumn (September) offer the best balance of good weather and fewer crowds.
- **For Festivals & Social Life**: Summer is unbeatable, though expect crowds.
- **For Romance & Quiet**: Autumn and winter deliver atmosphere, peace, and breathtaking scenery.
- **For Families**: Summer holidays bring the most options, though spring also works well if you want lambs and fewer crowds.

Final Word on Weather in the Dales

The Yorkshire Dales are known for being unpredictable when it comes to weather. A single day might start with sunshine, turn misty by noon, and bring light rain in the afternoon. This unpredictability is part of the charm—but it also means you should always come prepared. Waterproof clothing, good walking boots, and layered outfits are essential, no matter when you visit.

The bottom line: There is no "bad" time to visit the Yorkshire Dales—just different experiences waiting for you in each season.

2.2 Getting There & Around (Car, Train, Bus & Walking)

Reaching the Yorkshire Dales and moving around once you're here is part of the adventure. The landscape itself—rolling hills, winding lanes, stone bridges, and wide-open valleys—means that travel is never just about getting from A to B. Whether you're driving, taking the train, hopping on a local bus, or lacing up your boots for a long walk, each option offers its own experience of the Dales.

Getting to the Yorkshire Dales

The Yorkshire Dales are located in northern England, stretching across parts of North Yorkshire, Cumbria, and Westmorland. Their central position makes them surprisingly accessible from most major UK cities.

- **From London**: By train, you can reach Skipton or Settle in about 3–3.5 hours via Leeds. By car, the journey usually takes around 4–5 hours, depending on traffic.
- **From Manchester & Leeds**: Both cities act as gateways to the Dales. Manchester is about a 1.5–2-hour drive, while Leeds is even closer—about an hour by car. Train services from both cities are frequent and direct.
- **From Edinburgh or Glasgow**: Travelers from Scotland can reach the Dales in roughly 3.5–4.5 hours by car, or a similar time by train with a change at Leeds or Carlisle.

Arriving by train is often the most stress-free option, especially for those not used to driving on narrow country lanes. But if you want complete freedom to explore the more hidden corners, a car can be invaluable.

Getting Around the Dales by Car

Driving is the most flexible way to explore the Yorkshire Dales. Many of the villages, valleys, and remote walking spots aren't easily reached by public transport. With a car, you can take the scenic back roads, stop at viewpoints, and set your own pace.

That said, driving in the Dales comes with its quirks. Roads are often very narrow, sometimes reduced to single tracks with passing places. Stone walls and hedgerows can hug the edges tightly, leaving little room for error. Sheep wander freely across unfenced moorland roads, so patience is a must.

Parking is generally available in villages and at visitor centers, though some car parks charge a small fee. National Park car parks are well-signposted and usually close to major walking trails. If you're visiting during summer, expect busier roads, especially in popular spots like Malham, Aysgarth Falls, or Grassington.

For travelers renting a car, small or medium-sized vehicles are better suited to the Dales than large SUVs. They're easier to maneuver on the winding lanes and to fit into smaller parking areas.

Exploring by Train

If you love scenic rail journeys, the Yorkshire Dales are a dream destination. Two historic railway lines cut right through the region, offering some of the most beautiful train rides in the UK:

- **The Settle–Carlisle Railway**: Famous for its breathtaking views, this line runs north from Skipton and Settle, across the Ribblehead Viaduct, and into Cumbria. It's a journey that combines practicality with spectacle—you can use it to reach Dales villages or simply enjoy it as a sightseeing trip in its own right.
- **The Leeds–Morecambe Line**: Sometimes called "The Bentham Line," this route connects Leeds with Lancaster and Morecambe, passing through Skipton and smaller Dales towns. It's quieter but still full of charm.

Train stations in towns like Skipton, Settle, Garsdale, and Ribblehead can act as bases for walks. Many long-distance trails, such as the Dales Way, are designed to connect with train stations, making it easy to combine hiking with rail travel.

Buses: A Slower but Scenic Choice

Public buses run throughout the Dales, connecting larger towns and villages, but services are often infrequent. For travelers without a car, though, they can still be a good way to get around—especially in summer, when special "DalesBus" services run to popular hiking spots.

Buses are ideal for linear walks: you can start a trail in one village and finish in another, then catch a bus back. For example, you might walk from Malham to Settle or from Grassington to Burnsall, then rely on local transport to return.

If you're planning on using buses heavily, it's worth checking timetables in advance, as some routes run only a few times a day or not at all in winter.

Walking: The Heart of the Dales

Walking isn't just a way of getting around in the Yorkshire Dales—it's the best way to truly experience them. The National Park is crisscrossed with thousands of miles of public footpaths, bridleways, and long-distance trails. Some connect villages, while others take you across wild moorland or alongside rivers and waterfalls.

For short trips between villages, walking can sometimes be quicker than waiting for a bus. Trails are usually well-signposted, with iconic green waymarkers and stone stiles guiding the way. Many footpaths start right in the center of villages, so you can step out of your B&B and be on the trail within minutes.

Walking also connects you with the Dales' history—you'll find yourself following the same old packhorse routes, drovers' roads, and stone tracks that locals have used for centuries.

Blending Transport Options

For many visitors, the best way to explore the Yorkshire Dales is by mixing transport modes. You might:

- Take the train into Skipton, then rent a car for day trips.
- Use buses to link villages while relying on walking trails for the "in-between."
- Ride the Settle–Carlisle Railway for a scenic journey, then walk sections of the Dales Way directly from stations.

This mix allows you to balance flexibility with sustainability, reducing the environmental footprint of your visit while still enjoying the freedom to see remote corners.

Final Thoughts

Getting to and around the Yorkshire Dales isn't just about logistics—it's part of the adventure. A car gives you freedom, trains offer some of the most scenic journeys in Britain, buses connect communities in a slower but rewarding way, and walking remains the soul of the region. However you choose to travel, remember that the pace of life in the Dales is different. Roads are slower, distances feel longer, and sometimes a journey that looks short on a map can turn into an afternoon's exploration.

Take your time, embrace the slower rhythm, and let the journey become as memorable as the destination.

2.3 Travel Costs, Passes & Budgeting Tips

One of the questions most travelers ask before setting out on a trip to the Yorkshire Dales is simple: *how much will it cost me?* The good news is that the Dales can be enjoyed on almost any budget. Whether you want a shoestring hiking adventure, a mid-range countryside break, or a luxurious rural escape, the region is flexible. What makes the Dales particularly appealing is that many of its main attractions—its sweeping valleys, rugged fells, limestone cliffs, waterfalls, and picturesque villages—are completely free to visit.

That said, like any destination, the experience you have depends a lot on how you plan your spending. Costs vary depending on when you travel, how you get around, where you stay, and what kind of food and activities you prefer. Below is a clear look at what to expect, with tips to help you balance your budget without compromising on the magic of the Dales.

Accommodation Costs

Accommodation is likely to be the biggest expense. In larger towns like Skipton, Richmond, or Settle, you'll find a wider choice, while in tiny villages options can be limited and sometimes pricier due to high demand.

- **Budget stays**: Hostels and bunk barns are great for walkers and cyclists. They usually cost between **£20–£35 per night** for a dorm bed, and £40–£50 for a private room in a basic guesthouse. Camping is even cheaper, with many small farm campsites charging around **£10–£15 per person, per night**.
- **Mid-range**: Bed and breakfasts are the classic choice in the Dales. Expect to pay **£70–£110 per night** for a double room, often with a hearty Yorkshire breakfast included. This is excellent value since breakfast can keep you going well into the afternoon.
- **Luxury**: Country inns, boutique hotels, and converted manor houses cater to those seeking comfort. Prices here start at around **£150 per night** and can climb above **£250** in the most exclusive spots. The upside is often spa facilities, fine dining, or stunning historic settings.

Booking in advance is essential in peak summer (July–August) and during school holidays, as places fill quickly. If you're flexible, visiting in spring or autumn can save you 20–30% on accommodation costs.

Food & Drink

Food in the Yorkshire Dales can be as affordable or indulgent as you want it to be. Pub meals are an institution here, and they offer some of the best value for money.

- **Budget eating**: A pub lunch or light meal usually costs **£8–£12**, while hearty pub dinners (think pies, stews, or fish and chips) are **£12–£18**. Bakeries and farm shops are also fantastic for cheap, filling snacks.
- **Mid-range**: Local restaurants, gastropubs, or tea rooms often price mains between **£15–£25**. Afternoon tea, a very Yorkshire experience, typically costs **£15–£20 per person**.
- **Luxury dining**: For special occasions, the Dales boast several fine-dining restaurants and even Michelin-starred establishments. Expect to pay **£60–£90 per person** for a tasting menu.

One money-saving tip is to book self-catering cottages or stay somewhere with kitchen access. Supermarkets in market towns (Tesco, Co-op, Morrisons) let you cook for yourself, often at a fraction of the cost of eating out daily.

Transportation Costs

Getting around the Dales can be one of the trickier aspects of budgeting, especially if you don't drive.

- **By car**: Renting a car is the most flexible option. A compact hire car from Leeds or Manchester typically costs **£35–£50 per day**, plus fuel. Petrol in the UK averages about **£1.50–£1.60 per litre**, and because the Dales are quite rural, petrol stations can be sparse. Budget an extra **£30–£40 for fuel** if you're exploring for a few days.
- **By public transport**: Bus fares within the Dales average **£3–£7 per journey**, depending on distance. A day ticket for unlimited travel on certain routes can cost around **£10–£12**. Trains to gateway towns (like Skipton, Settle, or Ribblehead) vary widely in price: advance tickets from Leeds to Skipton can be as low as **£6–£8**, while last-minute fares may double.
- **Walking & cycling**: Once you're in the Dales, walking and cycling are free (aside from bike rental). A day's bike hire usually costs **£25–£35**, with electric bikes around **£40–£50**.

If you're planning to use public transport heavily, look into regional passes like the **Dales Rover Ticket**, which gives unlimited travel on selected bus and train routes across the Dales for a set daily fee.

Entrance Fees & Activities

Most of the highlights of the Yorkshire Dales—Malham Cove, Aysgarth Falls, Bolton Abbey, Ribblehead Viaduct—are free to access. However, some heritage sites and attractions do charge entrance fees.

- **Castles & abbeys**: Many historic sites cost between **£8–£15** per adult. English Heritage and National Trust members often get in for free.
- **Museums & visitor centres**: These usually charge modest fees of **£5–£10**, and some are free.
- **Adventure activities**: Guided caving, climbing, or outdoor tours usually cost **£40–£70 per person** for a half-day session.

If you're planning to visit multiple historic attractions, investing in a **National Trust membership (£84 per year)** or **English Heritage membership (£69 per year)** can save a lot, especially if you're touring other parts of the UK too.

Passes, Cards & Savings Tips

- **Railcards**: If you're traveling by train, UK railcards (like the **Two Together Railcard** or **16–25 Railcard**) save **1/3 off fares**. They cost about **£30 for the year**, but can pay for themselves in a single long journey.

- **Group travel**: Many local buses offer discounts for groups of 3–5 people traveling together.
- **Off-peak savings**: Traveling outside school holidays and weekends can reduce both accommodation and transport costs.
- **Free attractions**: Don't underestimate how much you can see without paying entry fees. The landscapes themselves are the stars of the show.

Average Daily Budget

To give you a ballpark idea, here's what different types of travelers might spend per day in the Yorkshire Dales (excluding flights to the UK):

- **Budget traveler**: £40–£60 (camping/hostel, self-catered meals, walking and free attractions, occasional bus fares).
- **Mid-range traveler**: £100–£150 (B&B, pub meals, car hire or train travel, a few paid attractions).
- **Luxury traveler**: £250+ (boutique hotels, fine dining, private tours, spa visits, and guided adventures).

Final Thoughts on Budgeting

The Yorkshire Dales don't demand extravagance to be rewarding. A simple picnic by a dry-stone wall, a walk through a sheep-dotted valley, or a wander around a historic market town costs little to nothing, yet often leaves the strongest memories. Still, knowing where to spend and where to save makes a big difference. If you put money into a comfortable base and a few special meals, balance it with free outdoor adventures, you'll get the best of both worlds: value for money *and* unforgettable experiences.

2.4 Sustainable & Responsible Travel

Traveling through the Yorkshire Dales is not just about admiring its beauty but also about protecting it. The rolling hills, stone-built villages, dry-stone walls, meadows, and wildlife you see today have been shaped over centuries by both nature and people. This landscape is fragile, and the way we travel can either support or harm it. Practicing sustainable and responsible travel ensures that the Dales remain just as stunning for future generations while also benefiting the local communities who live here.

Respecting the Landscape

The Dales are a working countryside where farmers, shepherds, and villagers live alongside wildlife and tourists. This means visitors have to tread with care. Staying on marked footpaths is more than just a suggestion—it helps prevent erosion, protects delicate wildflowers, and avoids disturbing livestock. For instance, sheep grazing on the hillsides are vital to the cultural character of the Dales, and stray dogs or careless hikers can easily disrupt their routine.

When walking or hiking, remember the countryside code: leave gates as you find them, avoid trampling crops or meadows, and take care near dry-stone walls. Many of these walls are centuries old, hand-built without mortar, and play an essential role in both history and farming. Leaning or climbing on them risks damage that takes hours of skilled labor to repair.

Supporting Local Communities

One of the best ways to travel responsibly in the Dales is by supporting the people who keep the area alive. Many of the villages here are small, with family-run pubs, guesthouses, and shops relying heavily on visitors. Choosing to buy local products—whether it's Yorkshire cheese, Dales wool, honey, or handmade crafts—not only gives you a more authentic experience but also helps sustain the rural economy.

Instead of always opting for chain hotels or supermarkets, staying in local inns, dining at village pubs, or visiting farmers' markets gives you a more memorable experience while ensuring your money stays in the community. It's also worth noting that some communities in the Dales are still recovering from economic challenges, and mindful tourism can make a real difference.

Reducing Your Environmental Impact

Cars are convenient for exploring the Dales, but they also contribute to traffic and pollution in areas not designed for heavy congestion. Choosing public transport where possible is a great alternative. The Settle–Carlisle railway line, for instance, is not only scenic but also eco-friendly compared to driving. If you do need a car, consider carpooling, renting an electric or hybrid vehicle, or planning your routes efficiently to minimize fuel use.

On the trails, remember the simple rule: "Leave no trace." This means carrying your litter with you, avoiding single-use plastics, and being mindful of what you bring into natural spaces. Even small actions, like carrying a reusable water bottle or coffee cup, can make a difference when thousands of visitors do the same.

Water is another area where visitors can be mindful. In dry summers, rivers and reservoirs in the Dales can come under stress. Using water responsibly—shorter showers, not wasting tap water in accommodations—helps preserve supplies for both locals and wildlife.

Protecting Wildlife

The Dales are home to unique bird species, including curlews, lapwings, and peregrine falcons. These species depend on quiet nesting grounds, and sometimes certain trails are closed during breeding season to protect them. Respecting these closures and keeping noise levels down helps ensure that these birds continue to thrive.

Wildflowers are another treasure of the Dales. Meadows full of orchids, buttercups, and gentians are rare in much of England but flourish here due to traditional farming practices. Picking wildflowers or disturbing these meadows can cause long-term damage. Instead, take photographs and leave nature as it is.

Traveling at a Gentle Pace

Responsible travel in the Dales is not about rushing from one attraction to another. It's about slowing down, soaking in the atmosphere, and recognizing that your visit fits into a much larger picture. Walking between villages, cycling on country lanes, or taking time to chat with locals at a tearoom is not just good for sustainability—it gives you a deeper connection to the landscape and its people.

Traveling slowly also spreads tourism more evenly. Many visitors flock to hotspots like Malham Cove or Aysgarth Falls, but the Dales are full of equally rewarding yet quieter corners. Exploring less-visited areas reduces pressure on popular trails while giving you a chance to experience solitude and authenticity.

Giving Back

Some visitors choose to take sustainability a step further by actively giving back. Volunteering with local conservation groups, donating to organizations that maintain trails, or even joining a guided walk run by the Yorkshire Dales National Park Authority are ways to contribute. These initiatives help maintain footpaths, protect wildlife habitats, and educate future visitors.

The Bigger Picture

Finally, sustainable travel in the Dales is also about mindset. It's about understanding that your presence has an impact, whether large or small, and choosing actions that benefit rather than harm. The Yorkshire Dales National Park was established to preserve this remarkable landscape for everyone to enjoy. Every traveler has a role in ensuring that its rivers remain clear, its hills unspoiled, and its villages thriving.

In essence, sustainable and responsible travel in the Yorkshire Dales is about balance: enjoying the freedom of open moorlands and quiet valleys while recognizing your role in protecting them. By traveling with care, you're not just a visitor—you're part of the story of the Dales, ensuring its legacy continues for generations.

3. Exploring the Dales: Towns & Villages

3.1 Grassington, Hawes & Reeth

The Yorkshire Dales is as much about its people and villages as it is about its sweeping hills and valleys. Scattered across the dales are communities that have held onto traditions, farming roots, and a pace of life that feels refreshingly different from the outside world. Among the most charming of these are **Grassington**, **Hawes**, and **Reeth**—each with its own character, history, and attractions. These towns are not only beautiful places to base yourself during a trip, but they also serve as living windows into the culture and heritage of the region.

Grassington: The Cultural Heart of Wharfedale

Grassington is often considered the beating heart of Wharfedale and one of the most popular villages for visitors. With its cobbled market square, honey-colored stone cottages, and lively atmosphere, it offers both the charm of a traditional Dales village and the convenience of modern visitor facilities.

History & Character

Grassington has roots that stretch back to the Bronze Age, but its golden age came in the 17th and 18th centuries with the boom in lead mining. The wealth generated by mining shaped much of the architecture you see today—sturdy stone houses, barns, and the well-laid square. Today, Grassington thrives as a hub for tourism, but it still retains a local feel, with independent shops, art galleries, and a strong community spirit.

Cultural Attractions

The town is home to the **Grassington Folk Museum**, a small but fascinating collection that tells the story of life in the Dales—everything from farming tools to tales of the lead miners. Each June, Grassington hosts the **Grassington Festival**, a two-week celebration of music, art, and performance that transforms the village into a stage. At Christmas, the **Grassington Dickensian Festival** brings the square alive with Victorian costumes, street performers, and festive markets.

Outdoor Access

Grassington sits on the **Dales Way**, a long-distance footpath that runs from Ilkley to the Lake District, making it a great base for walkers. Nearby, you'll find the dramatic limestone scenery of Grass Wood and Linton Falls, both easily accessible from the village on foot.

Accessibility in Grassington

Grassington is one of the better-equipped villages in the Dales for visitors with accessibility needs. The square is largely flat, though cobbles can be uneven for wheelchairs and pushchairs. The **National Park Visitor Centre** in Grassington offers accessible facilities, including step-free access, toilets, and mobility information. Some attractions, like the Folk Museum, are housed in historic buildings with limited access, but several cafes and pubs now offer level entry or ramps. For walkers, there are short, accessible routes from the village, including a path to Linton Falls that is suitable for those with limited mobility.

Hawes: A Market Town with a Proud Farming Heritage

If Grassington is about cultural events, Hawes is about living tradition. Located in Upper Wensleydale, this bustling market town is famous for its cheese, its market, and its lively sense of community.

History & Character

The name Hawes means "a pass between mountains," reflecting its position in the valley surrounded by high falls. It developed as a market town in the Middle Ages, with drovers bringing sheep and cattle to trade. That market tradition continues today, with the weekly **Tuesday market** still drawing locals and visitors. Hawes also became a key stop on the old coaching road between Lancaster and Newcastle, giving it a reputation for hospitality.

Cultural Attractions

The most famous attraction in Hawes is undoubtedly the **Wensleydale Creamery**, home of the world-famous Wensleydale cheese. Visitors can tour the creamery, watch cheese being made, and sample dozens of varieties. Nearby, the **Dales Countryside Museum**, located in a former railway station, offers deep insights into the heritage of the Dales—farming, crafts, and even stories of railway life.

Hawes is also known for its annual **Gala Day** and other agricultural shows, where sheepdog trials, local produce, and traditional skills are celebrated. These events give visitors a chance to connect with the authentic rhythms of rural life.

Outdoor Access

From Hawes, you're just a short walk from **Hardraw Force**, England's highest single-drop waterfall. The waterfall is set in a wooded gorge behind a historic pub, and it has inspired artists and musicians for centuries. Hawes is also on the **Pennine Way**, one of Britain's most famous long-distance walking trails, making it a key stop for hikers.

Accessibility in Hawes

Hawes is relatively accessible compared to some smaller villages. The **Wensleydale Creamery Visitor Centre** is wheelchair accessible, with lifts, wide doors, and accessible restrooms. The **Dales Countryside Museum** is also designed with accessibility in mind, offering level access, audio guides, and exhibitions that are easy to navigate. The weekly market, however, is held on uneven surfaces that may be challenging for wheelchairs. Paths to nearby attractions like Hardraw Force vary in difficulty; while the first section of the path is relatively smooth, the final approach involves steps and rough ground. Still, there are accessible walks nearby, including shorter riverside trails starting from the town.

Reeth: The Gateway to Swaledale

Reeth is smaller than Grassington or Hawes, but what it lacks in size it makes up for in setting and charm. Known as the gateway to Swaledale, it's a green village clustered around a triangular green, with sweeping views of the valley and moorland beyond.

History & Character

Reeth's story is deeply tied to the lead mining industry. In the 18th and 19th centuries, Swaledale was one of the richest lead mining areas in Britain, and Reeth was its heart. Miners once crowded the streets, and the remains of smelt mills and chimneys still dot the surrounding hillsides. When the mining declined, farming and tourism took over, but the character of the village—quiet, welcoming, and slightly rugged—remained.

Cultural Attractions

Reeth is home to the **Swaledale Museum**, a small but engaging collection about the area's mining heritage, rural life, and traditions. Each June, the village becomes the centre of the **Swaledale Festival**, a celebration of music, walking, and arts that attracts visitors from across the region. The village green is the focal point of community life, often hosting fairs, markets, and gatherings.

Outdoor Access

Reeth is surrounded by some of the most spectacular scenery in the Dales. From the village, footpaths lead directly into the hills, offering everything from short riverside strolls to challenging hikes over moorland. It's also a popular spot for cyclists tackling the **Tour de Yorkshire** routes or exploring the old mining tracks.

Accessibility in Reeth

Reeth is smaller and more traditional in layout, which means accessibility is more limited than in Grassington or Hawes. The village green itself is fairly level and provides good access to pubs, shops, and cafes, many of which are housed in old buildings with narrow doors and steps. The **Swaledale Museum** is set in a historic building and has partial accessibility, but space is tight for wheelchairs. Parking is available close to the green, making it easier for visitors with mobility needs. Accessible walking is more challenging here due to the steep and rugged nature of the valley, but there are short, flatter routes along the River Swale suitable for those who cannot manage the hills.

Comparing the Three

What makes these three towns stand out is how different they feel despite being part of the same region.

- **Grassington** is lively, cultural, and a hub for festivals and arts.
- **Hawes** is earthy, rooted in farming traditions and food culture.
- **Reeth** is quieter, more rugged, and steeped in mining history.

Together, they give a full picture of the Dales: community spirit, natural beauty, and living traditions. For accessibility, Grassington is the best equipped, followed by Hawes, while Reeth, though beautiful, is better suited to visitors who don't mind uneven ground.

3.3 Hidden Gems: Smaller Villages Worth a Stop

When people plan a trip to the Yorkshire Dales, names like Grassington, Hawes, or Skipton almost always come up first. But the Dales aren't just about the "big names." The real magic often lies in the smaller villages—the places where you'll find a single pub serving homemade pies, a tiny church that has stood for centuries, or a quiet green where sheep graze within sight of your picnic blanket.

Exploring these hidden gems adds depth to your journey. They aren't always easy to reach, but that's part of their charm. Below, we'll take you through some of the smaller villages that are worth slowing down for. Each offers something unique, whether it's dramatic scenery, historic sites, or a sense of timelessness you rarely find elsewhere.

Kettlewell – The Quintessential Dales Village

Nestled in Upper Wharfedale, Kettlewell looks almost like a movie set. Narrow stone streets weave between honey-colored cottages, and the River Wharfe tumbles gently through the village.

Why visit:

- Famous for its **Scarecrow Festival** each August, when villagers fill the lanes with witty, creative scarecrows.
- Stunning walking routes begin here, including hikes towards **Great Whernside** or gentler riverside strolls.
- Its old pubs, like the **Blue Bell Inn**, ooze character with open fires and hearty meals.

Getting there & accessibility:

- By car: Located on the B6160, best reached from Grassington (20 minutes). Roads are narrow and winding but scenic.
- By bus: DalesBus services connect Kettlewell to Grassington and Skipton on weekends and summer days.
- Accessibility: Streets are uneven, and parking is limited. Wheelchair access can be tricky in older pubs, though the riverside paths are flatter and easier.

Malham – A Natural Wonder Hub

Malham may be small, but its surroundings make it one of the most remarkable spots in the Dales. The limestone landscapes here—**Malham Cove, Gordale Scar, and Janet's Foss**—are icons of Yorkshire scenery.

Why visit:

- Malham Cove, a giant limestone cliff with a dramatic curved face. Its limestone pavement at the top was featured in *Harry Potter and the Deathly Hallows*.
- Gordale Scar, a hidden gorge with waterfalls cascading between towering cliffs.
- Janet's Foss, a fairy-like waterfall in a wooded glen.

Getting there & accessibility:

- By car: Around 6 miles from Settle via narrow lanes. Parking available at the village car park (paid).
- By bus: Seasonal buses run from Skipton and Settle.
- Accessibility: The village itself is small and walkable. Paths to Janet's Foss are moderate and uneven; Malham Cove involves steps. Gordale Scar is steep and challenging, but the village green and pubs are easily accessible.

Aysgarth – Home of the Famous Falls

Tucked in Wensleydale, Aysgarth is small, but its claim to fame is the **Aysgarth Falls**, a series of broad, stepped waterfalls along the River Ure.

Why visit:

- The falls are stunning in every season—thundering in spring, golden in autumn.
- Nearby woodlands make for relaxing walks.
- The village itself has peaceful green and traditional inns.

Getting there & accessibility:

- By car: On the A684, easy to reach from Leyburn or Hawes.
- By bus: Regular buses connect Leyburn, Hawes, and Bedale to Aysgarth.
- Accessibility: The falls have good footpaths, with some areas suitable for wheelchairs and pushchairs. A visitor center provides maps and facilities.

Middleham – Castles and Racehorses

Middleham is often called the "Newmarket of the North." It's a small town by size but feels like a large village with its market square and medieval castle.

Why visit:

- **Middleham Castle**, once home to Richard III. Its ruins are atmospheric and rich in history.
- The sight of **racehorses** being trained at dawn on the surrounding gallops is unforgettable.
- Quaint pubs and tea rooms offer a slower pace than nearby Leyburn.

Getting there & accessibility:

- By car: Just south of Leyburn via the A6108.
- By bus: Regular buses connect Leyburn and Ripon.
- Accessibility: Castle ruins involve uneven ground, though the village square and pubs are easy to navigate.

Dent – A Village Lost in Time

Dent sits in Dentdale, one of the quietest valleys in the Yorkshire Dales. Its cobbled streets and whitewashed cottages feel frozen in time.

Why visit:

- Known for **Dent Marble**, a type of decorative limestone.
- Home to the quirky **Dent Village Heritage Centre**.
- A base for peaceful walks with far fewer crowds.

Getting there & accessibility:

- By car: Narrow lanes lead into Dent from Sedbergh (around 5 miles). Driving requires care.
- By train: Dent Station, the highest mainline station in England, is 4 miles away on the Settle–Carlisle line. Taxis are limited, so plan ahead.
- Accessibility: The cobbled streets can be challenging for wheelchairs or prams, but the main green and pubs are manageable.

Masham – Art, and Sheep

Though a bit bigger than some villages, Masham is often overlooked compared to Ripon or Harrogate. It's famous for its breweries and sheep fairs.

Why visit:

- Home to **Theakston** and **Black Sheep Brewery**, both offering tours.
- Known for its **Sheep Fair**, celebrating the area's farming traditions.
- A lively market square and strong artistic community.

Getting there & accessibility:

- By car: Easily reached from Ripon or Bedale.
- By bus: Good bus links to Ripon, Bedale, and Leyburn.
- Accessibility: Flat market square makes it one of the more accessible places for wheelchairs and walkers.

Bolton Abbey – Riverside Charm

Bolton Abbey isn't a village in the traditional sense but a small hamlet and estate that has grown around the ruined priory.

Why visit:

- The **Bolton Priory ruins**, set against the River Wharfe, are breathtaking.
- Gentle riverside walks and the famous **stepping stones** across the river.
- Family-friendly trails and picnic areas.

Getting there & accessibility:

- By car: Just off the A59, easy access with large car parks.
- By bus: Services connect from Skipton and Ilkley.
- Accessibility: Excellent facilities with pushchair-friendly and wheelchair-friendly paths.

Practical Tips for Exploring Hidden Villages

- **Best way to explore:** Having a car gives the most flexibility, as bus services to small villages are often seasonal or limited.
- **Cycling:** The Dales are popular with cyclists, but be prepared for steep climbs and winding roads.
- **Walking:** Many of these villages are linked by long-distance walking routes such as the **Dales Way** or the **Pennine Bridleway**.
- **Parking:** Small villages often have very limited parking, so use official car parks when available.
- **Accessibility:** Larger villages and estate-managed sites (like Bolton Abbey) generally have better facilities for wheelchair users, while cobbled villages like Dent may pose challenges.

Why Hidden Villages Matter

Stopping in these smaller places is not just about sightseeing. It's also about supporting local communities. Every cup of tea in a village café or pint in a centuries-old pub helps sustain rural life in the Dales. Many of these villages have fewer than a few hundred residents, yet they maintain traditions, host festivals, and preserve the landscapes visitors come to enjoy.

Taking time to explore them deepens your connection to the Dales—it's not just about ticking off the "big sights" but about experiencing the quieter rhythms of Yorkshire life.

4. Natural Wonders & Top Attractions of the Dales

4.1 Famous Landscapes: Malham Cove, Gordale Scar & Ingleborough

Few places capture the dramatic essence of the Yorkshire Dales as vividly as **Malham Cove**, **Gordale Scar**, and **Ingleborough**. These natural wonders are not just geographical landmarks; they are icons that tell the story of ancient geology, ice-age forces, and the deep relationship between humans and the landscape. Visiting them is like stepping into a vast outdoor theatre, where cliffs, scars, caves, and towering peaks play the starring roles. Together, they make up the heart of any Dales adventure, each offering a completely different experience: Malham Cove with its striking limestone cliff and mysterious pavement, Gordale Scar with its raw, untamed gorge, and Ingleborough with its mountain presence dominating the horizon.

This section will guide you through these landscapes in depth—how to reach them, the best ways to explore, their history and geology, accessibility for different visitors, and the cultural meanings that have made them so beloved.

Malham Cove: A Natural Amphitheatre

Malham Cove is one of the most photographed and instantly recognisable features of the Yorkshire Dales. Imagine a towering **limestone cliff, 80 metres high and 300 metres wide**, curving like a crescent around a green valley. From a distance, it looks like a giant stone amphitheatre, but standing beneath it is an entirely different experience. The sheer vertical walls are dramatic, often streaked with water after rain, and the base is alive with birdsong and the bubbling stream of Malham Beck.

Geology and Formation

The cove is the legacy of the **last Ice Age**, around 12,000 years ago. As glaciers retreated, meltwater carved through the soft limestone, leaving behind this massive curved cliff. Above the cove lies a **limestone pavement**, one of the largest in Britain. Its clints (blocks) and grikes (fissures) create an otherworldly landscape—like walking on the back of a giant fossilised creature.

This pavement is more than just stone. It provides a microhabitat for rare plants such as ferns and alpine flowers, which grow in the sheltered grikes where soil and moisture collect. This delicate ecological system makes Malham a favourite with botanists and walkers alike.

Cultural and Literary Significance

Malham Cove has long captured human imagination. In the 19th century, it was painted and described by Romantic artists and poets, who saw in it the sublime power of nature. More recently, it featured in **Harry Potter and the Deathly Hallows (Part 1)**, where Harry and Hermione camp on the limestone pavement—bringing global recognition to this quiet corner of Yorkshire.

Exploring Malham Cove

- **Walking to the Cove**: Most visitors start from the village of **Malham**, a charming stone-built settlement about ¾ mile from the cove. The walk is relatively easy, following a well-maintained path along Malham Beck, and takes about 20–30 minutes.
- **The Limestone Pavement**: For those able to climb the 400+ stone steps to the top, the limestone pavement offers breathtaking views across the Dales. On a clear day, you can see Pen-y-ghent and the surrounding hills.
- **Birdlife**: Malham is also a hotspot for birdwatching. In spring and summer, look out for **peregrine falcons**, which nest on the cliffs. The RSPB often sets up telescopes near the base of the cove for visitors to observe these spectacular birds of prey.

Accessibility

For visitors with limited mobility, the lower path from Malham village to the base of the cove is **fairly level and wide**, suitable for pushchairs and off-road wheelchairs. The climb to the top, however, involves steep steps and uneven rock surfaces, which may not be suitable for everyone.

Gordale Scar: The Wild Gorge

If Malham Cove is a natural amphitheatre, then **Gordale Scar** is nature's cathedral—vast, vertical, and awe-inspiring. Just a short walk from Malham, this gorge has been described as one of the most dramatic sights in England. The sheer limestone cliffs rise nearly **100 metres**, enclosing visitors in a raw, rocky world that feels almost primeval.

Geological Origins

Like Malham Cove, Gordale Scar was formed by the erosive power of meltwater at the end of the Ice Age. Over thousands of years, torrents of water carved a deep gorge into the limestone, leaving behind this dramatic cleft. Two waterfalls tumble down its centre, fed by streams from Malham Tarn. In wetter seasons, the cascades roar; in summer, they shrink to a gentle trickle, revealing more of the rock formations.

The gorge's sheer scale has always inspired awe. Some historians believe it may have influenced early legends of giants or dragons in Yorkshire folklore.

Walking into Gordale Scar

The approach to Gordale Scar is part of its drama. From Malham, you can follow a riverside path through Gordale Beck, which leads you into the narrowing gorge. Suddenly, the cliffs close in, and the waterfalls appear ahead, framed by towering limestone walls.

For adventurous walkers, the route continues **up the waterfall itself**—a scramble that can be tricky and slippery, especially in wet conditions. Those less keen on climbing can simply enjoy the view from the base, which is spectacular in its own right.

Wildlife and Ecology

The damp, shaded walls of Gordale Scar provide a unique habitat for mosses, lichens, and ferns, some of which are rare in Britain. You may also spot dippers and wagtails flitting around the beck, while swallows nest in the cliff crevices.

Accessibility

The walk into the gorge from the roadside is relatively short (about 10–15 minutes), but the ground is uneven and rocky, making wheelchair access difficult. For those able to walk, it is one of the most rewarding short hikes in the Dales.

Ingleborough: The Iconic Peak

Standing at **723 metres (2,372 feet)**, **Ingleborough** is the second-highest mountain in the Yorkshire Dales and arguably its most famous. Its flat, table-like summit makes it instantly recognisable, and it has been a landmark for travellers for centuries. Together with Pen-y-ghent and Whernside, Ingleborough forms part of the legendary **Yorkshire Three Peaks Challenge**.

Geology and Landscape

Ingleborough's shape is the result of layered geology: limestone at the base, overlain by gritstone and millstone grit at the summit. This creates the mountain's distinctive terraced appearance. The lower slopes are dotted with caves, potholes, and shakeholes, making it a paradise for cavers and geologists.

On a clear day, the summit offers panoramic views stretching as far as the Lake District, Morecambe Bay, and even Snowdonia.

Human History and Archaeology

Ingleborough is not only a natural landmark but also a cultural one. Its summit hosts the remains of an **Iron Age hill fort**, suggesting it was once a place of ritual or defence. Ancient stone walls and circular foundations are still visible, a reminder that people have been drawn to this peak for millennia.

Walking Routes

- **From Clapham**: Perhaps the most popular route, starting from the village of Clapham. The trail passes through the **Ingleborough Estate Nature Trail**, past Ingleborough Cave and the dramatic ravine of Trow Gill.
- **From Horton-in-Ribblesdale**: Another well-trodden path, particularly for those tackling the Three Peaks Challenge. This is a steeper route, requiring good stamina.
- **From Ingleton**: A longer approach that gives walkers more time to appreciate the surrounding scenery.

Each route demands effort, but the reward is immense: the feeling of standing on top of one of Yorkshire's great natural monuments.

Accessibility

Ingleborough is a serious mountain hike, requiring good fitness, proper footwear, and preparation. It is **not suitable for wheelchairs or pushchairs**, and in poor weather it can be treacherous. For those seeking accessible viewpoints, nearby roads and lower-level walks offer excellent perspectives of the mountain without the strenuous climb.

Practical Tips for Visiting These Landscapes

1. **When to Visit:**

   - Spring and early summer bring wildflowers and nesting birds.
   - Autumn colours make the valleys glow.
   - Winter can be magical but requires caution, especially on Ingleborough.

2. **Transport & Access:**

   - Malham is reachable by car from Skipton or Settle, with parking available in the village.
   - Ingleborough is best accessed from Clapham, Horton-in-Ribblesdale, or Ingleton, all served by the Settle–Carlisle railway.
   - Local bus services connect some villages, though they are limited outside summer.

3. **Facilities:**

   - Malham village has pubs, tea rooms, and small shops.
   - Gordale Scar has limited facilities—bring water and snacks.
   - Clapham and Horton provide amenities for walkers heading up Ingleborough.

4. **Sustainability:**
   These landscapes are fragile. Stick to marked paths to protect rare plants, avoid littering, and respect local communities by keeping noise and traffic to a minimum.

Final Thoughts

Malham Cove, Gordale Scar, and Ingleborough are not just places to tick off on a sightseeing list—they are experiences that stay with you long after you leave. Malham's graceful amphitheatre inspires awe with its sheer beauty, Gordale Scar overwhelms with raw power, and Ingleborough challenges and rewards with its mountain majesty.

Together, they showcase the Yorkshire Dales at its most dramatic and most unforgettable.

For travellers, they offer a balance of accessibility and adventure: from gentle valley strolls to strenuous climbs, from family-friendly paths to scrambles up waterfalls. They are places where history, geology, and wildlife come together in a single, breathtaking landscape. To stand at the foot of Malham Cove, within the shadow of Gordale Scar, or on the summit of Ingleborough is to feel a deep connection—not just to the Yorkshire Dales, but to the enduring forces of nature itself.

4.2 Waterfalls: Aysgarth Falls, Hardraw Force & Hidden Streams

The Yorkshire Dales is as much about its **rushing waters and tumbling falls** as it is about its rolling hills and limestone cliffs. Waterfalls here are not only scenic spots but also deeply tied to the history, culture, and ecology of the region. Some are easy to reach by car or short walks, making them accessible for families, while others reward those who lace up their boots and head into quieter corners of the valleys. In this section, we'll explore the **famous cascades of Aysgarth and Hardraw**, as well as **lesser-known streams and hidden gems** that you can discover off the beaten path.

Aysgarth Falls: Beauty in Three Steps

Arguably the most famous waterfall in the Yorkshire Dales, **Aysgarth Falls** is a series of three broad cascades on the River Ure near the village of Aysgarth in Wensleydale. These falls have been admired for centuries; even Wordsworth and Turner drew inspiration from their beauty, and they famously appeared in *Robin Hood: Prince of Thieves* (1991).

- **The Three Falls**:
    - **Upper Falls** – closest to the visitor centre, with a wide curtain of water tumbling over limestone steps.
    - **Middle Falls** – a little quieter, great for photos with fewer crowds.
    - **Lower Falls** – more rugged and dramatic, surrounded by woodland.
- **Accessibility & Trails**:
    - A **well-maintained path** leads to viewpoints of the Upper Falls, suitable for families and those with limited mobility.

- o The full walk along the River Ure linking all three falls is about **2 miles round trip**. Sturdy footwear is recommended as the paths can be muddy.
- **Facilities**:

  - o Aysgarth Falls National Park Centre has **parking, toilets, and a café**, making this one of the more visitor-friendly waterfall stops.
  - o Dogs are welcome, but should be kept on leads due to livestock in nearby fields.
- **Best Times to Visit**:

  - o After rainfall, when the falls are at their most powerful.
  - o Early mornings or evenings in summer to avoid crowds.
  - o Autumn offers stunning colours in the surrounding woodland.

Hardraw Force: England's Highest Single Drop

Tucked away behind the **Green Dragon Inn** in the village of Hardraw, **Hardraw Force** is a dramatic single-drop waterfall plunging 100 feet into a rocky amphitheatre. It holds the title of the **tallest unbroken waterfall in England**, and its enclosed gorge-like setting gives it a unique, almost theatrical feel.

- **Visiting the Falls**:

  - o Access is via the **Green Dragon Inn**, where visitors pay a small fee to walk through the garden and into the gorge.
  - o The walk is short and flat, making it relatively accessible.
- **Experience & Atmosphere**:

  - o The gorge is cool, damp, and shaded, creating a natural "cathedral" with mossy walls and echoing sound.
  - o The waterfall freezes in winter during cold snaps, creating spectacular ice formations.
- **Cultural Notes**:

  - o The setting has inspired artists and musicians, and it hosts the **annual Brass Band Festival**, where the natural acoustics create a magical outdoor concert experience.
  - o It was also used as a film location for *Robin Hood: Prince of Thieves*.
- **Tips for Visitors**:

  - o Combine your trip with a hearty pub lunch at the Green Dragon.

- Wear sturdy shoes, as the path can be slippery.
- Expect larger crowds in summer, but quieter visits in spring or autumn.

Hidden Streams & Lesser-Known Falls

Beyond the headline attractions, the Dales hides countless smaller streams and waterfalls. These **"secret" cascades** often lie just off walking trails and reward those willing to explore.

- **Cautley Spout (near Sedbergh)**

    - One of the highest waterfalls in England (though technically in the Howgills, at the edge of the Dales).
    - Best seen after heavy rain, as it splits into dozens of rivulets tumbling down a steep hillside.
    - Accessible via a challenging walk from Sedbergh or the Cross Keys Inn.
- **Janet's Foss (near Malham)**

    - A charming woodland waterfall said to be home to a fairy queen named Janet.
    - Surrounded by lush greenery, it feels enchanting, especially in spring.
    - Easily reached via a short walk from Malham village, often combined with hikes to Malham Cove and Gordale Scar.
- **Cotter Force (near Hawes)**

    - A wide, stepped waterfall hidden in woodland.
    - Notably, it has a **wheelchair-accessible path**, making it one of the most inclusive waterfall experiences in the Dales.
    - Quiet and peaceful compared to the busier Aysgarth.
- **Mill Gill Force (near Askrigg)**

    - A short walk from Askrigg leads to this dramatic two-tiered fall tucked away in a wooded gorge.
    - Ideal for a quick detour if you're exploring Wensleydale.
- **West Burton Falls (Cauldron Falls)**

    - Located right in the village of West Burton, this small but lovely waterfall is nicknamed "Cauldron Falls" for the way water swirls in the pool below.
    - Easily accessible and great for photos, especially after rain.

Seasonal Experiences

Waterfalls in the Dales change dramatically with the seasons:

- **Spring**: Snowmelt swells rivers, making waterfalls roar with life. Bluebells and wild garlic carpet nearby woodlands.
- **Summer**: Falls may shrink in drier weather, but warmer days make for pleasant hikes and picnics.
- **Autumn**: Rich colours in the trees frame the cascades, creating stunning photo opportunities.
- **Winter**: Some falls freeze into icy curtains – magical but requiring extra care when visiting.

Travel & Accessibility Tips

- **Getting There**:

    - Most major waterfalls (Aysgarth, Hardraw, Janet's Foss) can be reached by car, with parking nearby.
    - Public buses connect Aysgarth and Hawes, though timetables can be limited, especially on weekends.
    - For hidden waterfalls, walking is often the only way – plan routes in advance using an OS map or local walking app.
- **Accessibility**:

    - Aysgarth Falls and Cotter Force offer wheelchair-friendly paths.
    - Others, like Hardraw Force, involve short but uneven ground.
    - More remote waterfalls such as Cautley Spout require steep climbs and are not suitable for limited mobility.
- **Safety**:

    - Rocks around waterfalls are **very slippery** – good boots are essential.
    - Avoid swimming unless clearly permitted, as currents can be dangerous.
    - Respect private land and follow marked paths.

Why Waterfalls Matter

The waterfalls of the Yorkshire Dales are not just tourist spots – they are **natural sculptures shaped by time, geology, and weather**. They inspire art, literature, and local folklore. They provide habitats for rare mosses, ferns, and insects. And for visitors, they offer moments of stillness, beauty, and awe. Whether you're standing before the roaring drama of Hardraw Force, wandering through the magical woods to Janet's Foss, or stumbling upon a hidden cascade by chance, these falls are reminders of the power and peace of water in the Dales.

4.3 Geological Marvels: Ribblehead Viaduct, White Scar Cave & Limestone Pavements

The Yorkshire Dales is often celebrated for its sweeping valleys, rolling green fields, and charming villages, but beneath its gentle beauty lies a landscape shaped by immense geological forces. The area's ancient limestone, carved by water, time, and human ingenuity, has created some of the most striking landmarks in England. From the engineering wonder of the **Ribblehead Viaduct**, to the hidden depths of **White Scar Cave**, and the otherworldly patterns of **limestone pavements**, this corner of the Dales offers a fascinating glimpse into the region's natural and human history.

Ribblehead Viaduct: Engineering Amidst the Fells

Standing in the open expanse of Batty Moss, the **Ribblehead Viaduct** is not just a railway bridge—it's a symbol of Victorian ambition and endurance. Built between 1870 and 1874 as part of the Settle–Carlisle Railway, the viaduct stretches 400 meters across the valley with 24 soaring stone arches, each reaching up to 32 meters in height.

The construction was no small feat. Thousands of workers, known as navvies, toiled in harsh conditions, often battling cold, rain, and disease. Many lived in makeshift camps around the site, and tragically, hundreds are thought to have died during the project. Today, their memory lingers in local graveyards and in the sheer presence of the viaduct itself, which seems to blend seamlessly into the rugged hills.

The Ribblehead Viaduct remains a working railway, carrying passenger trains along one of Britain's most scenic routes. Visitors can admire the structure from the ground, walk across the moorland paths surrounding it, or even ride the train for sweeping views across the Dales. In winter, when snow dusts the fells, the viaduct takes on an especially dramatic atmosphere, while summer brings blooming wildflowers to the surrounding moors.

- **Getting There:** The viaduct is accessible via the **Ribblehead railway station** (on the Settle–Carlisle line), making it easy for travelers without a car. For drivers, parking is available at the Station Inn, a traditional pub just a short walk away. Walking trails from here lead to excellent vantage points.

- **Accessibility:** While the rough moorland terrain may pose challenges for wheelchairs, the area around the Station Inn provides some flatter ground with good viewing opportunities.

White Scar Cave: A Journey Beneath the Dales

While the Ribblehead Viaduct dominates the landscape above, the **White Scar Cave**, near Ingleton, reveals the hidden world beneath. It is the longest show cave in Britain, stretching more than four miles, with around a mile open to the public on guided tours.

The cave was discovered in 1923 by Christopher Long, a Cambridge student who crawled through a small passage and stumbled upon an underground wonderland. Today, visitors follow in his footsteps, guided through chambers filled with stalactites, stalagmites, and fascinating formations created by thousands of years of water dripping through limestone.

Highlights include:

- **The Battlefield Cavern**, one of the largest underground chambers in Britain, measuring 90 meters long and 15 meters high.
- **The Devil's Tongue**, a striking stalactite formation.
- **The Witch's Fingers**, strange finger-like rocks.

As guides share stories of geology and folklore, you gain an appreciation of the patience of nature—how mineral-rich water slowly carves and decorates these subterranean spaces over millennia.

- **Visiting Details:** Tours last about 80 minutes and require sturdy footwear, as paths can be damp and uneven. The cave maintains a cool temperature year-round, so warm clothing is recommended even in summer.

- **Accessibility:** The initial section of the cave involves low ceilings and uneven ground, making it unsuitable for wheelchairs and difficult for those with mobility issues. However, for those able to manage, the guides provide an informative and safe experience.

- **Getting There:** White Scar Cave is about a 10-minute drive from Ingleton village, with car parking available onsite. Public buses to Ingleton operate from Lancaster, Kirkby Lonsdale, and Settle, though onward travel to the cave itself may require a taxi or local walk.

Limestone Pavements: Nature's Sculpture Gardens

Perhaps the most iconic geological feature of the Yorkshire Dales is its **limestone pavements**—flat expanses of exposed limestone crisscrossed by natural fissures called *grikes*, with blocks of stone between them known as *clints*. These pavements were shaped during the last Ice Age, when glaciers stripped away soil and vegetation, leaving bare limestone exposed to the elements. Over thousands of years, rainwater dissolved the rock, carving the deep cracks and jagged formations we see today.

The most famous example lies above **Malham Cove**, where the limestone pavement creates an otherworldly landscape that looks almost like a giant chessboard. Walking across it is both exhilarating and humbling: plants like ferns and small trees grow in the grikes, finding shelter from wind and grazing animals, while the flat clits provide sweeping views across the Dales.

Other notable pavements include:

- **Scales Moor near Ingleborough** – dramatic pavements with far-reaching views.
- **Great Asby Scar National Nature Reserve** – a more remote site, less visited but equally spectacular.

These pavements are ecologically important, supporting rare flora such as hart's-tongue fern, rock rose, and limestone bedstraw. Their unusual beauty has also made them famous on screen—Malham's pavement was featured in *Harry Potter and the Deathly Hallows*.

- **Getting There:** Malham is accessible by car (with parking in the village), and buses run from Skipton. From the village, the pavement is reached by a steep but rewarding hike up to Malham Cove. Ingleborough and Scales Moor pavements are best accessed by footpaths starting in nearby villages such as Ingleton or Horton-in-Ribblesdale.

- **Accessibility:** Limestone pavements are uneven, rocky, and often slippery in wet weather, making them unsuitable for wheelchairs or those with limited mobility. However, accessible viewing areas of Malham Cove itself allow many visitors to enjoy the scenery without tackling the full climb.

Bringing It All Together

The Ribblehead Viaduct, White Scar Cave, and limestone pavements tell three different but connected stories of the Yorkshire Dales: the determination of humans to conquer the landscape, the hidden artistry of nature beneath the surface, and the slow power of geology shaping the land itself. Together, they showcase why the Dales is more than just rolling hills—it is a living classroom of history, science, and wonder.

Whether you're an engineer admiring Victorian design, a geologist tracing the path of ancient glaciers, or simply a traveler seeking awe-inspiring sights, these marvels of stone and time will leave a lasting impression.

4.4 Valleys & Countryside Charm: Swaledale, Wensleydale & Wharfedale

One of the greatest joys of exploring the Yorkshire Dales is wandering through its valleys — known locally as *"dales"* — where lush meadows, winding rivers, stone walls, and scattered villages create postcard-perfect views. Among the many dales, three stand out for their beauty, history, and accessibility: **Swaledale**, **Wensleydale**, and **Wharfedale**. Each has its own personality, and together they capture the heart of the Dales experience.

Swaledale: Rugged Beauty & Sheep-Dotted Hills

Swaledale is often considered the wildest and most unspoiled of the Yorkshire Dales. Named after the River Swale, which cuts through its dramatic valley, this dale is known for its **heather-covered moors**, **stone barns**, and **dry-stone walls** that zigzag across the hillsides.

- **Landscape & Scenery**
  Swaledale is breathtaking in every season. In spring, lambs bounce in the fields; in summer, meadows burst with wildflowers; in autumn, the heather paints the hills purple; and in winter, the valley can look like something from a storybook under a dusting of snow.

- **Villages & Market Towns**
  The dale's heart is **Reeth**, a village that feels timeless with its wide green, stone cottages, and local pubs. It's a hub for walkers and cyclists, with trails heading into the surrounding fells. Another gem is **Muker**, particularly famous in late June and July when its hay meadows are alive with orchids, buttercups, and other rare wildflowers.

- **Things to Do in Swaledale**

    - **Hiking & Walking**: The Coast to Coast trail passes through here, offering spectacular routes. Local circular walks take you along the river, up onto the moors, or through hay meadows.
    - **Lead Mining History**: Swaledale was once a center for lead mining. The **Swaledale Museum in Reeth** tells this story, and you can also see atmospheric ruins of old mine buildings scattered across the hills.
    - **Cycling**: Swaledale became famous during the 2014 Tour de France's Yorkshire Grand Départ. Today, keen cyclists can follow those same routes.

- **Accessibility & Getting There**
    Swaledale is reached by road, with scenic drives from Richmond or Aysgarth. The roads are narrow in places but manageable for most vehicles. Buses run from Richmond to Reeth, though services are limited, so planning ahead is key.

Wensleydale: Waterfalls, Cheese & Gentle Green Valleys

If Swaledale is wild and rugged, **Wensleydale** is softer, greener, and famous for its cheese. Unlike most dales, it isn't named after its river (the River Ure flows here) but after the village of Wensley.

- **Landscape & Scenery**
    Wensleydale's beauty lies in its gentle green pastures, rolling hills, and scattered waterfalls. Dry-stone walls frame every view, while sheep graze peacefully in fields that look like patchwork quilts from above.

- **Highlights of Wensleydale**

    - **Aysgarth Falls**: A three-tiered series of waterfalls, popular with painters, poets, and even Hollywood (they appeared in *Robin Hood: Prince of Thieves*).
    - **Hardraw Force**: England's highest single-drop waterfall, tucked behind the Green Dragon Inn.
    - **Bolton Castle**: A mighty medieval fortress near Leyburn, once the prison of Mary Queen of Scots.
    - **Wensleydale Creamery in Hawes**: The birthplace of the famous Wensleydale cheese, loved by Wallace & Gromit. Visitors can tour the creamery, sample cheeses, and even watch cheesemakers at work.

- **Hawes**: The bustling market town at the dale's heart, full of tearooms, craft shops, and traditional inns. Market day (Tuesdays) brings it especially to life.
- **Activities in Wensleydale**

    - **Walking**: Trails lead to waterfalls, across meadows, and along the Pennine Way, which passes through Hawes.
    - **Heritage Railways**: The **Wensleydale Railway** offers nostalgic steam and diesel train rides through the countryside.
    - **Food & Drink**: Beyond cheese, the dale is home to traditional bakeries, farm shops, and cozy pubs serving hearty Yorkshire fare.
- **Accessibility & Getting There**
 Wensleydale is one of the most accessible dales, with Hawes connected by good roads to Leyburn, Richmond, and Sedbergh. Bus services run from Northallerton, Richmond, and Leyburn to Hawes, making it more reachable by public transport compared to some other valleys.

Wharfedale: Riverside Villages & Walking Paradise

Named after the River Wharfe, **Wharfedale** is a dale of contrasts, stretching from the bustling market town of Otley in the south to wild moorland in the north. It's beloved by walkers thanks to its long riverside paths, historic villages, and easy connections to the outside world.

- **Landscape & Scenery**
 Wharfedale blends dramatic scenery with pastoral charm. The lower dale features woodlands, rolling hills, and riverside paths, while the upper dale (around Kettlewell and Buckden) feels more remote and rugged. The River Wharfe itself is a constant companion, its clear waters winding gracefully through fields and villages.

- **Villages & Towns**

    - **Grassington**: Perhaps the most charming town in Wharfedale, Grassington has cobbled streets, art galleries, independent shops, and lively festivals, including a Dickensian Christmas Market.
    - **Kettlewell**: A pretty village surrounded by fells, known for its quirky annual scarecrow festival.
    - **Burnsall**: A picture-perfect riverside village with a stone bridge and riverside walks.

- ○ **Ilkley**: Famous for Ilkley Moor (immortalized in the song "On Ilkla Moor Baht 'at"), its spa-town atmosphere, and stylish shops.
- **Things to Do in Wharfedale**

    - ○ **Walking**: Wharfedale is paradise for walkers. The **Dales Way** long-distance trail follows the river from Ilkley all the way to the Lake District, passing through the dale's prettiest villages.
    - ○ **Cycling**: Scenic routes take cyclists up challenging climbs and across beautiful moorland.
    - ○ **Fishing & Nature**: The River Wharfe is popular for fishing, and its banks are great for spotting kingfishers, herons, and otters.
    - ○ **Historic Houses & Gardens**: Nearby attractions include **Bolton Abbey,** a ruined priory surrounded by woodland and riverside walks. Families love the stepping stones across the river.
- **Accessibility & Getting There**
  Wharfedale is one of the easiest dales to reach. Regular trains run to Ilkley from Leeds and Bradford, making it a great starting point for those relying on public transport. Buses connect Ilkley and Grassington, while drivers can explore the upper dale by scenic minor roads.

Comparing the Three Dales

- **Swaledale**: Wild, rugged, and perfect for those seeking solitude and traditional landscapes.
- **Wensleydale**: Green, welcoming, and full of waterfalls, cheese, and family-friendly attractions.
- **Wharfedale**: Accessible, varied, and a great introduction to the Dales, especially for walkers.

Practical Tips for Exploring the Valleys

- **Best Time to Visit**: Late spring and early summer bring wildflowers and long daylight hours; autumn offers golden colors; winter is quieter but can be magical with frost or snow.
- **Getting Around**: A car gives maximum freedom, but many bus routes connect the villages, especially in summer. Walking is the best way to appreciate the details of the countryside.
- **What to Pack**: Waterproofs and good walking boots are essential, as weather can change quickly. Bring a picnic to enjoy by the riverside or in one of the meadows.

In short: Swaledale, Wensleydale, and Wharfedale are the beating heart of the Yorkshire Dales. Each offers something unique — from Swaledale's rugged beauty, to Wensleydale's waterfalls and cheese, to Wharfedale's riverside charm and walking trails. Visiting all three gives travelers the complete Dales experience.

4.5 Wildlife & Nature Reserves

The Yorkshire Dales may be best known for its limestone cliffs, dramatic valleys, and iconic green pastures, but its **wildlife and protected reserves** are just as enchanting. From soaring birds of prey to delicate orchids tucked away in meadows, this region is alive with biodiversity. The national park and its surrounding conservation areas provide some of the UK's most important habitats, making it a paradise for **wildlife lovers, photographers, and anyone who enjoys quiet moments in nature**.

In this section, we'll explore the remarkable wildlife you can expect to see in the Dales, highlight key **nature reserves**, and provide practical guidance on how to experience these places responsibly.

Wildlife of the Dales: What You Might See

The Dales' varied landscapes—limestone pavements, upland heaths, hay meadows, rivers, and wetlands—support an extraordinary mix of species.

- **Birdlife:**
  The skies are often filled with **curlews**, their haunting calls echoing across the moors, or the bubbling songs of **lapwings** in spring. High above, you might spot a **red kite** gliding gracefully or even a **peregrine falcon** swooping across cliffs. In the moorlands, keep an eye out for **grouse**, especially around August during the heather bloom. Rare species such as the **black grouse** also cling to isolated areas, though sightings require luck and patience.

- **Mammals:**
  While the Dales is not home to large wild mammals like deer in abundance, there are charming species such as **otters**, which can occasionally be seen along rivers like the Wharfe. **Hares** dart across upland fields, while **badgers** and **foxes** emerge at dusk. If you're especially lucky, you might even glimpse a **stoat in its white winter coat**.

- **Flora:**
  The Dales are a hotspot for wildflowers. In early summer, the **traditional hay**

meadows—some of the richest in England—burst into life with buttercups, daisies, cranesbill, and orchids. These meadows, carefully preserved by farmers and conservationists, are a living window into Britain's agricultural past. On limestone pavements, look out for rare species like **maidenhair spleenwort** or the delicate **alpine cinquefoil**.

- **Insects & Butterflies:**
  The meadows and moorlands are also alive with buzzing pollinators, including the endangered **northern brown argus butterfly**, found in a few pockets of the park. Bees and dragonflies thrive in the Dales' wetlands, adding even more life to summer walks.

Key Nature Reserves in the Yorkshire Dales

1. **Malham Tarn National Nature Reserve**

   - Located near the famous Malham Cove, Malham Tarn is one of only two natural lakes in the Yorkshire Dales. It is also a **Site of Special Scientific Interest (SSSI)**, recognized for its unique wetlands, fens, and limestone habitats. The tarn is home to **rare plants**, dragonflies, and a rich bird population, including **great crested grebes** and **reed buntings**. The surrounding trails are accessible and perfect for families, with interpretive signs explaining the natural history of the area.

2. **Ingleborough National Nature Reserve**

   - Stretching around the slopes of Ingleborough, this reserve covers limestone pavements, caves, meadows, and heaths. It's a hotspot for **botanists and geologists** alike. Orchids thrive in the meadows during summer, while peregrine falcons and ravens nest on the cliffs. It's one of the best places in the Dales to experience the interplay between geology and ecology.

3. **Grass Wood Nature Reserve** (near Grassington)

   - A rare ancient woodland in the Dales, Grass Wood is a magical place for those who enjoy peaceful walks under a leafy canopy. In spring, the woodland floor is carpeted with **bluebells**, while the trees echo with the song of warblers and woodpeckers. It's a great contrast to the open moorland scenery most visitors associate with the Dales.

4. **Gait Barrows National Nature Reserve** (on the edge of the Dales)

- Though just outside the park's boundary, this reserve is worth the detour. Known for its limestone pavements and rich wildlife, it harbors species such as the **Duke of Burgundy butterfly** and unusual plants. Its combination of rare geology and biodiversity makes it a favorite with nature enthusiasts.

5. **Yockenthwaite Meadows & Muker Meadows**

    - For traditional hay meadows, few places are as beautiful as those in **Swaledale and Wharfedale**. In June and July, these meadows become a kaleidoscope of color and fragrance. Farmers still use traditional mowing techniques here, ensuring these precious habitats are preserved. These meadows also offer one of the best opportunities for **wildflower photography** in the UK.

Seasonal Highlights for Wildlife Watching

- **Spring:** Migratory birds return, meadows bloom, and rivers run with activity. Otters are more visible at dawn and dusk.
- **Summer:** Butterflies and orchids reach their peak. Hay meadows glow golden with wildflowers, and skylarks fill the air with song.
- **Autumn:** Fungi appear in woodlands, berries attract flocks of thrushes, and moorlands glow purple with heather.
- **Winter:** Harsh but beautiful. Look for hares in white pelts and the haunting silhouettes of raptors hunting in open skies.

Accessibility & Visitor Tips

- **Wheelchair-Friendly Trails:** Malham Tarn has some **accessible pathways** around the lake, and parts of Grass Wood are suitable for visitors with limited mobility.
- **Best Times to Visit:** For birdwatching, spring and early summer are ideal. For flowers, late June is the peak meadow season.
- **Guided Walks:** The Yorkshire Dales National Park Authority and organizations like the **Yorkshire Wildlife Trust** run guided walks and wildlife events, which are perfect if you want expert insight.
- **What to Bring:** Binoculars, a camera with zoom, and good footwear are must-haves. In summer, insect repellent will come in handy.
- **Responsible Travel:** Stick to paths to avoid trampling delicate plants, never disturb nesting birds, and take litter home. Dogs should be kept on leads during nesting season to protect ground-nesting birds.

Why It Matters: Conservation in the Dales

Many of the species and habitats in the Dales are under threat from modern farming practices, climate change, and human pressure. Conservation programs, supported by the **Yorkshire Dales National Park Authority**, the **RSPB**, and local farmers, work tirelessly to balance human activity with nature preservation. By visiting these reserves and supporting local initiatives, travelers play a role in keeping the Dales wild and vibrant for future generations.

In summary: The wildlife and reserves of the Yorkshire Dales aren't just an optional extra—they're central to the region's identity. Whether you're spotting peregrines on the cliffs of Malham, photographing wildflowers in Swaledale, or quietly listening for curlews on a summer evening, the Dales offer countless opportunities to connect deeply with nature.

5. Outdoor Adventures

5.1 Walking & Hiking Trails for All Levels

One of the greatest joys of visiting the Yorkshire Dales is lacing up your boots and stepping into landscapes shaped by nature and history. From gentle riverside strolls to challenging mountain scrambles, the Dales offers trails that suit every type of walker—families with children, casual ramblers, seasoned hikers, and long-distance trekkers alike. Walking here isn't just about exercise; it's about experiencing rolling valleys, dramatic limestone cliffs, waterfalls hidden in woodlands, centuries-old dry-stone walls, and wildlife that brings the countryside alive.

The Dales are part of England's rich walking tradition, with footpaths that date back hundreds of years. Many routes were once drovers' tracks used to move sheep and cattle, or packhorse trails linking villages long before modern roads existed. Today, those routes have been preserved and marked, ensuring walkers can follow in the footsteps of generations past while enjoying the beauty of protected landscapes.

To help you make the most of your walking adventures, this guide breaks down trails into three categories: **easy walks for beginners and families, moderate rambles**

for those seeking variety, and **challenging treks for experienced hikers**. Alongside the trails, you'll find practical tips on maps, signage, seasonal conditions, accessibility, and safety, so you're fully prepared for your adventure.

A. Easy & Family-Friendly Walks

These routes are perfect for beginners, families with children, or anyone who wants to enjoy the scenery without tackling steep climbs. They usually take between 1–3 hours, follow clear paths, and often feature picnic spots, tea rooms, or villages nearby.

1. Malham Village to Janet's Foss (2 miles / 3 km round trip)

- **Highlights**: Woodland paths, a magical waterfall named after a woodland fairy, and a flat trail suitable for most abilities.
- **Why walk it**: This gentle stroll is like stepping into a fairytale. The shaded woodland feels worlds away from the open dales, and children love the story of Janet, the Queen of the Fairies, said to live in the waterfall's cave.

2. Grassington Riverside Walk (3 miles / 5 km loop)

- **Highlights**: Meadows, the River Wharfe, Linton Falls, and charming village streets.
- **Why walk it**: An ideal introduction to the Dales, this walk combines riverside calm with the bustle of Grassington village. The waterfalls at Linton are especially photogenic after rain.

3. Aysgarth Falls Woodland Walk (2 miles / 3 km round trip)

- **Highlights**: Upper, Middle, and Lower Aysgarth Falls; easy woodland paths; picnic areas.
- **Why walk it**: A perfect family trail. Each set of waterfalls offers a different view, and you can watch the River Ure crash dramatically over limestone steps.

4. Reeth to Grinton (2 miles / 3.5 km one way)

- **Highlights**: Easy stroll linking two villages, views across Swaledale, pubs and tearooms at both ends.
- **Why walk it**: A simple way to enjoy village life. Families can even make this walk part of a day out by exploring Reeth's green or visiting Grinton's historic church.

B. Moderate Walks (Half-Day Adventures)

These routes involve more varied terrain, occasional steep sections, and longer distances (5–10 miles / 8–16 km). They are perfect for walkers who want a challenge but not a full-day expedition.

1. Malham Cove & Gordale Scar Loop (7.5 miles / 12 km loop)

- **Highlights**: The dramatic cliffs of Malham Cove, the hidden waterfall at Gordale Scar, Janet's Foss, and panoramic views from the limestone pavement above the cove.
- **Why walk it**: This is one of the most famous walks in the Dales, combining three geological wonders into one loop. The variety—woodlands, cliffs, waterfalls, and open countryside—makes it unforgettable.

2. Bolton Abbey & The Strid (6 miles / 10 km loop)

- **Highlights**: The ruins of Bolton Priory, riverside paths, and the dramatic Strid gorge where the River Wharfe squeezes into a narrow chasm.
- **Why walk it**: A mix of history and nature. The abbey ruins are atmospheric, and the riverside paths are stunning in spring when wildflowers bloom.

3. Hawes to Hardraw Force (5 miles / 8 km round trip)

- **Highlights**: A lively market town, England's highest single-drop waterfall, and countryside fields.
- **Why walk it**: This is a short but rewarding walk that combines village charm with natural spectacle. Hardraw Force tumbles dramatically into a wooded gorge and is especially powerful after heavy rain.

4. Grassington to Conistone Pie (6 miles / 9.5 km loop)

- **Highlights**: Limestone outcrops, sweeping views across Wharfedale, and the unusual hill formation known as Conistone Pie.
- **Why walk it**: A quieter walk compared to Malham but just as scenic. The hilltop views make it a favorite for photographers.

C. Challenging Hikes (Full-Day Treks & Classic Routes)

For experienced walkers with good fitness and proper gear, the Dales offers some of the UK's most iconic hikes. Expect distances of 10–25 miles, steep climbs, rugged terrain, and some navigational challenges. The rewards are immense: panoramic views, high peaks, and the satisfaction of tackling legendary trails.

1. The Yorkshire Three Peaks Challenge (24 miles / 39 km loop)

- **Route**: Pen-y-ghent → Whernside → Ingleborough → back to Horton-in-Ribblesdale.
- **Highlights**: Three of the Dales' highest peaks, limestone pavements, Ribblehead Viaduct, and sweeping 360° views.
- **Why walk it**: This is the ultimate Dales challenge. Many hikers aim to complete it within 12 hours, but even if it takes two days, it's a bucket-list experience.

2. Ingleborough from Clapham (10 miles / 16 km loop)

- **Highlights**: Show caves like Ingleborough Cave, Trow Gill gorge, Gaping Gill (a vast natural pothole), and summit views.
- **Why walk it**: This route combines underground wonders with mountain scenery. Standing on Ingleborough's flat-topped summit feels like being on the roof of the Dales.

3. Great Shunner Fell from Hawes (13 miles / 21 km round trip)

- **Highlights**: One of the highest peaks in the Dales, wild moorland, and spectacular views into both Swaledale and Wensleydale.
- **Why walk it**: A quieter but equally rewarding alternative to the Three Peaks. The open landscapes feel wonderfully remote.

4. Wharfedale Three Peaks (14 miles / 23 km loop)

- **Route**: Birks Fell → Buckden Pike → Great Whernside.
- **Highlights**: Less crowded than the famous Yorkshire Three Peaks, but still a major challenge with rewarding panoramas.
- **Why walk it**: Ideal for hikers seeking a demanding but quieter adventure.

D. Long-Distance Trails

The Yorkshire Dales is also crisscrossed by national trails and long-distance footpaths for multi-day walking holidays.

- **The Pennine Way**: Britain's first official long-distance path runs through the Dales, including the section from Malham to Horton-in-Ribblesdale, considered one of its highlights.
- **The Dales Way**: A 78-mile trail from Ilkley to the Lake District, following riverside paths and valleys, suitable for walkers who enjoy long but gentle walking.
- **The Coast-to-Coast Walk**: Created by Alfred Wainwright, this famous trail crosses the Dales between Reeth and Kirkby Stephen.

- **The Herriot Way**: A 50-mile circular route inspired by the beloved vet James Herriot, showcasing Swaledale and Wensleydale.

E. Practical Walking Advice

Maps & Navigation

- Carry an **Ordnance Survey map** (OL2, OL30, OL19 depending on the area) or a reliable GPS app like OS Maps or AllTrails.
- Waymarks are common, but fog and moorland can be disorienting.

Best Seasons

- **Spring**: Wildflowers, baby lambs, and milder weather.
- **Summer**: Longer daylight hours, but busier trails.
- **Autumn**: Golden landscapes and fewer crowds.
- **Winter**: Atmospheric, but prepare for snow, ice, and short daylight hours.

Gear

- Waterproof boots, layered clothing, rain jacket, and walking poles for steep or rocky terrain.
- Pack snacks, water, and emergency supplies (whistle, torch, first aid kit).

Accessibility

- Some routes like **Aysgarth Falls** and parts of **Bolton Abbey** have accessible paths for wheelchairs and pushchairs.
- National Park visitor centers often provide accessibility guides.

Safety

- Check weather forecasts before setting out (conditions change quickly).
- Always let someone know your route if heading into remote areas.
- Be mindful of livestock, keep dogs on leads, and follow the **Countryside Code**.

Final Thoughts on Walking in the Dales

Walking in the Yorkshire Dales is more than following a path—it's about slowing down and connecting with the land. You might pause to watch a shepherd guide his flock, admire the craftsmanship of a centuries-old dry-stone wall, or listen to the bubbling of a river as you eat your packed lunch. Whether you're tackling a mighty peak or meandering beside a stream, every walk tells a story of nature and history intertwined.

The beauty of the Dales is its inclusivity: you don't need to be an elite hiker to enjoy its trails. With routes ranging from short family strolls to marathon challenges, everyone can find their own adventure here. And once you've experienced it, the call of the Dales will almost certainly bring you back for more.

5.2 Cycling & Mountain Biking Routes

The Yorkshire Dales is often called **Britain's cycling heartland**, and for good reason. With quiet country lanes winding through stone-walled fields, legendary climbs that test even seasoned riders, and rugged trails crisscrossing wild moorlands, the Dales offers some of the finest cycling in the UK. Whether you're looking for a peaceful family ride along riverside paths or an adrenaline-pumping mountain bike challenge, you'll find routes that fit every level.

Cycling here is more than just exercise—it's about **immersing yourself in the landscape**. Each ride brings new sights: dry-stone barns scattered across meadows, waterfalls tumbling after rain, and grazing sheep that seem to eye cyclists with mild curiosity. Add to that the friendly welcome in Dales villages, where you can stop for tea and scones or a hearty pub lunch, and you'll see why the Dales is a bucket-list destination for cyclists.

Road Cycling in the Dales

The Dales shot to international cycling fame after hosting the **2014 Tour de France Grand Départ**, and since then, the region has been a magnet for road riders. Expect long climbs, thrilling descents, and sweeping valley views that make the effort worthwhile.

Iconic Road Climbs

- **Buttertubs Pass (between Swaledale and Wensleydale):**
  Perhaps the most famous climb in the Dales, Buttertubs is a steep, winding ascent that rewards riders with extraordinary views. It's a tough challenge, but reaching the top is unforgettable.

- **Fleet Moss (near Hawes):**
  Known as one of the highest roads in Yorkshire, this climb takes you into remote moorland with sweeping panoramas. The descent into Wharfedale is exhilarating

but requires care due to sharp bends.

- **Park Rash (near Kettlewell):**
  Short but brutally steep, this climb tests stamina and determination. The sharp gradient at the start makes it one of the most demanding roads in the Dales.

- **Tan Hill (near Reeth):**
  The road to Tan Hill Inn, Britain's highest pub, is a classic ride. The steady climb takes you through wild landscapes where you may feel like the only person for miles.

Leisure & Family Road Routes

Not all road cycling in the Dales is about punishing climbs. There are also **gentle valley rides** that follow rivers and meander through pretty villages.

- **The Swale Trail (Reeth to Keld):**
  A family-friendly, mostly off-road trail with smooth surfaces that follows the River Swale. It's perfect for children or beginners.

- **The Wensleydale Loop (Hawes – Aysgarth – Bainbridge):**
  A moderate circular route that passes waterfalls, villages, and meadows. It combines manageable terrain with lots of interesting stops along the way.

- **Dales Cycleway (130-mile circuit):**
  This long-distance road cycling route loops through many valleys and scenic passes, offering a "grand tour" of the Yorkshire Dales. Many cyclists complete it over several days.

Mountain Biking in the Dales

For off-road riders, the Dales is a paradise of **bridleways, moorland tracks, forest trails, and technical descents**. The rugged limestone terrain and natural features create a mix of flowy sections and rocky challenges.

Popular MTB Areas & Trails

- **Swaledale:**
  Known for its mix of singletrack and moorland bridleways. Trails near Reeth and Fremington Edge offer thrilling climbs and descents, with stunning views across

the valley.

- **Settle & Malham:**
  Limestone landscapes around Malham Tarn and Mastiles Lane provide exciting, rocky routes. Mastiles Lane, a Roman road turned bridleway, is a classic for mountain bikers.

- **Ingleborough Area:**
  Trails around Ingleton and Clapham lead into technical limestone terrain and rugged uplands. White Scar Cave and Ingleborough add a dramatic backdrop.

- **Nidderdale (Area of Outstanding Natural Beauty):**
  Though just outside the core National Park, Nidderdale offers superb MTB routes like Scar House Reservoir trails, with challenging climbs and rewarding scenery.

Technical Trails vs. Easy Rides

- **Easy/Moderate MTB:**
  The Swale Trail is the best choice for beginners and families—it's off-road, safe, and scenic.
  Green and blue-graded routes near Grassington also suit riders who want manageable terrain.

- **Challenging MTB:**
  Advanced riders can tackle **The Fremington Edge Loop** in Swaledale, known for steep climbs and rocky descents. Another demanding option is the **Settle Loop**, part of the Pennine Bridleway, which mixes tough terrain with incredible limestone views.

Long-Distance Cycling & Touring

The Dales is also a dream for those who love **multi-day cycle touring**.

- **Way of the Roses (170 miles, Morecambe to Bridlington):**
  This coast-to-coast route passes through Settle and the heart of the Dales, with some of the region's finest views.

- **Pennine Bridleway (South to North):**
  Designed for both mountain bikers and horse riders, this trail includes the Settle

Loop and continues through rugged Pennine landscapes.

- **Yorkshire Dales Cycleway (130 miles):**
  A full circuit of the National Park, best split over 4–6 days. Each section highlights a different dale, giving a complete cycling experience of the region.

Cycling Events in the Dales

If you'd like to ride with a community of cyclists, the Dales hosts a number of popular events:

- **Etape du Dales:** A challenging sportive with over 100 miles of climbing and descending through the toughest Dales passes.
- **Three Peaks Cyclo-Cross:** The world's toughest and oldest cyclo-cross event, covering the Yorkshire Three Peaks (Pen-y-ghent, Whernside, and Ingleborough).
- **Local Sportives:** Throughout the summer, smaller organized rides take place in different valleys, welcoming both experienced cyclists and casual riders.

Practical Tips for Cycling in the Dales

- **Bike Hire & Shops:** Rental bikes (road, mountain, and e-bikes) are available in villages like Hawes, Ingleton, Reeth, and Skipton. Local shops also offer repairs.
- **E-Bikes:** Electric bikes are becoming popular for tackling steep Dales climbs. Many hire shops now provide e-MTBs and e-road bikes.
- **Weather:** Conditions change quickly. Always bring layers, waterproofs, and lights—even in summer.
- **Navigation:** Many bridleways are unmarked; GPS devices or detailed maps (OS Explorer series) are essential for off-road riding.
- **Respect Trails:** Stick to designated bridleways and paths. Some footpaths are off-limits to bikes.
- **Fuel Stops:** Tearooms, pubs, and village shops make great rest points—many are cyclist-friendly and provide secure bike storage.

Why the Dales is a Cyclist's Dream

What makes the Dales special for cycling isn't just the routes—it's the **combination of scenery, solitude, and culture**. One moment you're grinding up a steep pass surrounded by windswept moorland, the next you're freewheeling into a valley dotted with stone cottages and hearing church bells ring. It's this mix of challenge and charm that keeps cyclists coming back.

Whether you're an experienced rider looking to conquer famous climbs or a family seeking a relaxed riverside pedal, the Yorkshire Dales offers unforgettable journeys on two wheels.

5.3 Caving, Climbing & Adventure Sports

The Yorkshire Dales is not just a place for peaceful strolls and scenic drives—it is also one of the **UK's most exciting adventure playgrounds**. Beneath its rolling hills lies one of Europe's most extensive cave systems, while its cliffs, crags, and limestone escarpments challenge climbers of every ability. Add in adrenaline-fuelled activities like canyoning, potholing, abseiling, and gorge scrambling, and you'll see why the Dales attract outdoor enthusiasts from all over the world.

1. Caving in the Yorkshire Dales

The Dales is widely regarded as the **caving capital of Britain**. Its unique limestone geology has created a labyrinth of underground passages, caverns, waterfalls, and potholes formed over millions of years. Whether you're curious about exploring a beginner-friendly showcave or eager to take on a serious potholing expedition, the Dales has something to offer.

Showcaves for Visitors (Accessible to All)

If you're new to caving or simply want a family-friendly underground adventure, the Dales boasts several **showcaves** that are safe, guided, and lit for visitors:

- **White Scar Cave (near Ingleton)**
  The longest showcave in Britain, stretching over a mile underground, White Scar offers a breathtaking journey through enormous caverns, underground waterfalls, and striking formations like stalactites and stalagmites. The highlight is the **Battlefield Cavern**, one of the largest cave chambers in the UK. Guided tours run daily and provide fascinating insights into geology and local folklore.

- **Ingleborough Cave (Clapham)**
  Situated at the base of Ingleborough, one of the Dales' iconic Three Peaks, Ingleborough Cave is renowned for its impressive formations, crystal-clear streams, and easy accessibility. A well-lit path allows visitors of all ages to enjoy the subterranean beauty.

- **Stump Cross Caverns (near Pateley Bridge)**
  A magical showcave system filled with stalactite-lined chambers and a strong

sense of history—prehistoric bones have been discovered here. Educational displays make this an excellent option for families and school groups.

These showcaves are ideal starting points for understanding the Dales' underground world before progressing to more challenging pursuits.

Wild Caving & Potholing Adventures

For the adventurous, the Dales is home to **over 2,500 known caves** and potholes, making it a mecca for wild caving. Many of these systems remain connected, with networks stretching for miles underground.

- **Gaping Gill (Clapham)**
  Perhaps the most famous pothole in Britain, Gaping Gill is an enormous chamber where **Fell Beck stream plunges 98 metres** into the darkness below—the highest unbroken waterfall in England. The main chamber is so large that **St Paul's Cathedral could fit inside**. Access is usually only possible with specialist clubs, but twice a year, local caving clubs set up winch meets, allowing the public to descend into this awe-inspiring void.

- **Alum Pot (near Selside)**
  Another dramatic pothole, Alum Pot features vertical shafts, waterfalls, and vast underground caverns. It requires rope techniques (SRT – single rope technique) and is suitable only for experienced cavers or those on guided trips.

- **Ease Gill Caverns**
  With around **60 kilometres of passages**, Ease Gill is the longest cave system in Britain. A mixture of crawling passages, underground rivers, and decorated chambers makes it a destination for serious cavers.

- **Langcliffe Pot & Mossdale Caverns**
  For the highly experienced, these are challenging systems known for their difficulty and commitment. Mossdale Caverns, in particular, has a notorious reputation for flooding hazards and should never be attempted without expert knowledge.

Guided Caving Experiences

If you're a beginner but eager to experience **real caving**, several outdoor centres and guides in the Dales provide safe introductions:

- **Lost Earth Adventures** (based in Yorkshire) offer guided caving trips ranging from beginner explorations to full-day potholing expeditions.
- **Yorkshire Dales Guides (Settle)** provide highly trained instructors who tailor trips for all levels.
- **Ingleborough Cave & Adventure Centres** in Clapham also run sessions ideal for school groups, families, and first-timers.

Expect to crawl, climb, squeeze through passages, and see underground waterfalls and unique rock formations. Helmets, lamps, and protective equipment are usually provided.

2. Rock Climbing in the Dales

Above ground, the Yorkshire Dales is equally famous for its **rock climbing**. Its limestone cliffs and gritstone crags offer routes for beginners and seasoned climbers alike.

Classic Climbing Locations

- **Malham Cove**
  World-famous in the climbing community, Malham's massive limestone amphitheatre is a hotspot for sport climbing. It offers some of the hardest routes in the UK, attracting elite climbers from around the globe. Names like "Raindogs" and "Overshadow" are legendary within the sport.

- **Gordale Scar**
  This dramatic gorge isn't just for walkers—it's also home to some excellent climbing routes, with steep limestone faces and overhangs.

- **Kilnsey Crag**
  Another iconic limestone cliff, Kilnsey is known for its huge overhangs and technical challenges. The 40-metre-high crag dominates Wharfedale and provides dozens of demanding sport climbs.

- **Almscliff Crag (near Harrogate)**
  A gritstone outcrop that offers a very different experience from limestone. With a mix of bouldering and trad climbing routes, it's a favourite for climbers in Yorkshire.

- **Twistleton Scar & Giggleswick Scar**
  These are more beginner-friendly options, with plenty of shorter routes and

bolted climbs suitable for novices.

Climbing Styles in the Dales

- **Sport Climbing** – Concentrated around Malham, Kilnsey, and Gordale. Bolted routes allow climbers to push their limits on some of the hardest climbs in the UK.
- **Trad Climbing** – The gritstone edges, including Almscliff, provide endless trade opportunities, where climbers place their own protection.
- **Bouldering** – Popular at Brimham Rocks and Almscliff, offering low-level climbing without ropes, using crash pads.
- **Winter Climbing** – In cold winters, waterfalls and damp crags sometimes freeze, allowing rare opportunities for ice climbing.

Indoor Climbing Options

If the weather turns (as it often does in Yorkshire), indoor climbing centres provide excellent training and fun:

- **Kendal Wall** (just outside the Dales in Cumbria)
- **Harrogate Climbing Centre**
- **Ingleton Climbing Wall**

These centres cater to all ages and abilities.

3. Adventure Sports Beyond Caving & Climbing

The Yorkshire Dales has much more to offer for thrill-seekers:

- **Canyoning & Gorge Scrambling**
  Descend rivers and waterfalls with ropes, jumps, and slides. Locations like **Ghyll Scrambling in Swaledale** and **canyoning in How Stean Gorge** are especially popular.

- **Abseiling**
  Many cliffs and viaducts in the Dales are used for abseiling experiences. Instructors often set up ropes at sites like **Brimham Rocks** and **How Stean Gorge**, giving beginners a taste of controlled descents.

- **Via Ferrata (How Stean Gorge)**
  Unique in Yorkshire, How Stean Gorge offers a via ferrata course—metal ladders

and bridges fixed into the gorge walls, similar to Alpine adventures.

- **Zip-Lining & High Ropes**
  Centres like **How Stean Gorge** also feature high ropes courses and zip-lines, great for families and groups.

- **Adventure Racing & Endurance Events**
  The Dales host adventure races, orienteering challenges, and ultra-marathons, often combining running, biking, and kayaking.

4. Safety, Equipment & Practical Tips

Caving, climbing, and adventure sports can be dangerous without proper preparation. Here are key tips:

- **Go with a Guide** if you're inexperienced. The Dales have many local operators who ensure safety.
- **Check the Weather** – Rain can quickly flood caves and make climbing routes dangerous.
- **Wear Proper Gear** – Helmets, harnesses, lamps, ropes, and waterproof clothing are essential.
- **Know Your Limits** – The Dales offer both beginner-friendly activities and extreme challenges. Don't push beyond your experience level.
- **Respect Nature** – Many caves and crags are home to bats and rare plants; avoid disturbing them.
- **Plan Ahead** – Cell service is poor in many valleys. Inform someone of your plans before heading out.

5. Who Are These Adventures For?

- **Families** – Showcaves, abseiling, and beginner gorge scrambling.
- **Beginners** – Guided caving, climbing schools, and indoor climbing walls.
- **Experienced Adventurers** – Malham Cove, Gaping Gill, and Alum Pot.
- **Thrill Seekers** – Canyoning, via ferrata, and adventure races.

6. Why the Yorkshire Dales is Special for Adventure

Unlike other parts of Britain, the Yorkshire Dales combines **world-class climbing**, **record-breaking caves**, and **unique gorge experiences** in one region. You can spend the morning descending into an underground waterfall, the afternoon scaling a crag above Wharfedale, and the evening enjoying a pint in a centuries-old inn. This blend of wild nature, geological wonders, and welcoming culture makes the Dales a truly exceptional destination for adrenaline-fuelled adventure.

6. Cultural Experiences & Heritage

6.1 Castles, Abbeys & Historic Sites

The Yorkshire Dales is more than just sweeping valleys and outdoor adventures—it's also a place where history lives on in stone walls, ruined abbeys, and grand castles. As you travel through the Dales, you'll find medieval fortresses perched on hilltops, romantic abbey ruins hidden in meadows, and historic houses that reveal how people lived through the centuries. Visiting these sites offers not only a window into the past but also some of the most atmospheric settings in England.

Bolton Castle

One of the best-preserved medieval castles in England, **Bolton Castle** sits proudly above Wensleydale near the village of Redmire. Built in the late 14th century by Richard le Scrope, the castle has an impressive history—it once held **Mary, Queen of Scots**, prisoner in 1568. Today, the castle is partly a ruin but much of it remains intact, allowing visitors to climb towers, walk along battlements, and explore medieval kitchens and chambers. Regular events bring history to life, from falconry displays to reenactments of Tudor life. The views from the castle across Wensleydale are breathtaking, especially at sunset.

Skipton Castle

Known as the "gateway to the Dales," **Skipton Castle** is a magnificent, fully roofed fortress that has stood for over 900 years. Unlike many castles in Britain, Skipton has survived wars and time remarkably well. Visitors can wander through banqueting halls, dungeons, and the original chapel. Its sturdy walls and defensive towers tell stories of sieges during the English Civil War, while its interior shows how a castle transformed into a comfortable residence over the centuries. Families especially enjoy the atmospheric walk through its medieval rooms and leafy courtyard.

Middleham Castle

Middleham may look like a ruined shell at first glance, but this historic site has a special place in English history. Known as the "Windsor of the North," **Middleham Castle** was the childhood home of **Richard III**. The remains are expansive, and climbing the castle's keep provides sweeping views over Wensleydale. Interpretation boards and exhibitions help you imagine life during the Wars of the Roses. The charming village of Middleham, with its cobbled streets and famous horse-racing stables, makes the visit even more rewarding.

Jervaulx Abbey

Peaceful, atmospheric, and partially hidden by nature, **Jervaulx Abbey** is one of the most romantic ruins in the Dales. Once home to Cistercian monks, the abbey was dissolved during Henry VIII's Reformation, leaving behind haunting stone arches and ivy-clad walls. Unlike many historic sites, Jervaulx Abbey is privately owned and maintained as an **"open ruin,"** meaning you can wander freely among the stones at your own pace. The surrounding wildflowers, birdsong, and gentle setting give it a truly magical feel—especially at dawn or dusk.

Fountains Abbey & Studley Royal

Though technically on the edge of the Yorkshire Dales, **Fountains Abbey** is a UNESCO World Heritage Site and one of the most spectacular monastic ruins in England. The massive Cistercian abbey, founded in 1132, stretches dramatically across the valley, with towering columns and vast cloisters. Next door lies **Studley Royal Water Garden**, a masterpiece of 18th-century landscape design with ornamental lakes, statues, and hidden follies. Together, the abbey and gardens make for an unforgettable day trip, blending medieval devotion with Georgian elegance.

Rievaulx Abbey

Another remarkable abbey within easy reach of the Dales, **Rievaulx Abbey** was one of the first Cistercian monasteries in England. Its soaring ruins sit in a tranquil valley, giving visitors a sense of the scale and importance of monastic life in the Middle Ages. Today, it's managed by English Heritage and includes a fascinating visitor centre with exhibits on abbey life. The combination of dramatic ruins and peaceful surroundings makes it a favorite with photographers and history lovers alike.

Historic Churches & Chapels

Scattered across the Dales are dozens of historic churches and chapels that reflect centuries of rural faith. **St. Mary's Church in Muker**, for example, is a simple yet beautiful 16th-century church in the heart of Swaledale. **St. Margaret's Church in Hawes** has ties to medieval pilgrims and is still a vibrant community hub. Many churches feature **Anglo-Saxon stone carvings**, Norman arches, or Victorian stained glass, rewarding visitors who step inside.

Practical Tips for Visiting Historic Sites

- Many castles and abbeys are **managed by English Heritage or the National Trust**, so consider membership if you plan multiple visits.
- **Opening hours** vary seasonally; some sites close in winter or have reduced access.
- Wearing sturdy shoes—castles and abbeys often involve uneven steps, grassy ruins, and stone floors.
- Bring a camera—whether it's the dramatic silhouette of a castle tower or the delicate detail of a carved abbey column, these places are photogenic in every season.
- Some sites, like **Jervaulx Abbey**, operate on an **honesty box system** for donations, so carry some coins or small notes.

In short, the castles, abbeys, and historic sites of the Yorkshire Dales tell stories of power, faith, and resilience. From the grandeur of Skipton Castle to the haunting ruins of Jervaulx and Fountains Abbey, each stop adds a layer of depth to your journey through the Dales—making history as much a part of your adventure as the landscapes themselves.

6.2 Museums & Folk Traditions

The Yorkshire Dales isn't just about breathtaking landscapes and outdoor adventures—it's also a land steeped in history, culture, and community traditions that have been passed down for centuries. If you want to truly understand the heart of the Dales, step inside its small but fascinating museums, and don't miss the folk customs and rural practices that still shape life here today. These experiences provide a window into the lives of the farmers, miners, artisans, and villagers who have called this rugged yet beautiful region home.

Museums of the Dales

The Yorkshire Dales is dotted with intimate, locally run museums that reveal the region's layered past. Unlike the vast national institutions in London, these museums feel personal, often housed in old schools, mills, or cottages. They are rich with stories of resilience, industry, and community life.

- **Dales Countryside Museum (Hawes)** – Located in the old Hawes railway station, this is perhaps the most comprehensive museum in the Dales. Here, you can explore everything from Bronze Age tools to displays about sheep farming, mining, and the lives of Victorian families. There are reconstructed workshops showing blacksmithing, rope-making, and quilting, giving you a sense of how self-sufficient these communities once were. The museum often hosts demonstrations and seasonal exhibitions, making it a lively stop for families and **history lovers alike.**

- **Craven Museum & Gallery (Skipton)** – Situated inside Skipton Town Hall, this museum blends archaeology, textiles, natural history, and local crafts. Its collection includes the famous Shakespeare First Folio, as well as displays on prehistoric finds, Roman artifacts, and Victorian clothing. It gives visitors a broad understanding of the cultural richness of the Dales, and because it's in Skipton, it makes a perfect companion visit to the medieval Skipton Castle nearby.

- **Swaledale Museum (Reeth)** – This tiny but deeply charming museum is community-run and tells the story of lead mining, rural trades, and farming in Swaledale and Arkengarthdale. Exhibits include everything from butter churns to miners' lamps, reminding you how hard but meaningful life was in these valleys. The volunteers here are incredibly knowledgeable, often sharing personal stories passed down through generations.

- **Richmondshire Museum (Richmond)** – Known for its quirky and nostalgic displays, this museum includes a recreated grocer's shop, chemist's shop, and lead-miner's cottage. It even features a set from the beloved British TV series *All Creatures Great and Small*, which was filmed in the area. For fans of literature and TV, it's a particularly fun stop.

- **Grassington Folk Museum** – Tucked into a 17th-century building, this museum is a time capsule of everyday village life. You'll find displays of farming tools, domestic objects, and costumes, all telling the story of how people lived, worked, and celebrated in the Dales.

- **Dent Village Heritage Centre (Dentdale)** – Dentdale is known as the birthplace of geologist Adam Sedgwick, and its museum explores both his life and the broader history of this secluded valley. Exhibits also highlight "terrible knitters of Dent," the skilled but notoriously strict knitters who once produced woolens for the whole region.

Each of these museums has its own personality, but they share one thing in common: they're run with passion, often by locals who see themselves as custodians of their community's story. Visiting them gives you a chance to not just see artifacts, but to connect with people whose families have lived here for centuries.

Folk Traditions of the Yorkshire Dales

Beyond the walls of museums, the Dales is alive with traditions and folk customs—some centuries old, others evolving with time. These customs reflect the agricultural rhythms of the land and the strong community spirit of rural villages.

- **Agricultural Shows & Sheepdog Trials** – Across the Dales, summer brings country shows where farmers display their best livestock, compete in sheepdog trials, and take part in dry-stone walling competitions. The Kilnsey Show, for example, is one of the biggest, featuring not only animals but local crafts, music, and fell races. These events are a wonderful way to experience rural pride and community gathering.

- **Folk Music & Dance** – Traditional folk music has deep roots in the Dales. Violins, accordions, and flutes once filled village pubs during gatherings, and that tradition continues today in folk clubs and at festivals like the Swaledale Festival or Grassington Festival. Morris dancing, with its bright costumes and bells, can also occasionally be seen during fairs and celebrations.

- **Seasonal Customs** – In villages like Dent and Muker, remnants of ancient customs remain. Harvest festivals, Maypole dancing, and Christmas mummers' plays all hint at how communities once celebrated the cycles of the year. Some villages still hold lantern parades or carol singing events that feel timeless.

- **Craft Traditions** – Hand-knitting, quilting, and woodworking have long been staples of the Dales. In the past, knitting wasn't just a hobby but an economic necessity, particularly in Dentdale, where families knit for income. Quilting, too, was a prized skill, with quilts often made for weddings or passed down as heirlooms. Today, local craft fairs and heritage days celebrate these traditions, and you can often find handmade goods for sale in village shops.

- **Storytelling & Dialect** – The Dales has a strong oral tradition, with tales of lead-mining ghosts, local heroes, and mischievous spirits passed down through generations. The Yorkshire dialect itself is part of this cultural fabric—though softened in modern times, you may still hear older residents using traditional words and phrases unique to the area.

Why It Matters

Exploring museums and folk traditions in the Yorkshire Dales isn't just about looking at objects behind glass—it's about stepping into a living story. These places and practices bring depth to your visit, turning a landscape of valleys and hills into a human story of survival, community, and creativity. Whether you're listening to folk music in a village hall, watching a sheepdog trial, or wandering through a heritage museum, you'll feel the heartbeat of the Dales in ways that hiking alone can't provide.

Travel Tip: Pair your museum visits with local events. For instance, visit the Swaledale Museum during the Swaledale Festival, or stop by the Dales Countryside Museum when it hosts heritage craft demonstrations. It's the perfect way to see history come alive.

6.3 Local Festivals, Events & Fairs

The Yorkshire Dales is not just about sweeping landscapes and charming villages—it is also a land rich with traditions, seasonal celebrations, and lively community gatherings that bring its history and culture to life. From centuries-old agricultural shows to modern food and music festivals, these events provide travelers with a unique window into the heart and soul of Dale's life. Attending a local festival is one of the best ways to experience the warmth, humor, and hospitality of the people who live here.

1. Agricultural Shows – A Celebration of Rural Life

Agricultural shows are a cornerstone of Dale's culture, reflecting the region's deep connection to farming and countryside traditions. They often feature livestock competitions, traditional craft displays, local produce stalls, and even sheepdog trials. These events attract farmers, families, and visitors alike, creating a true sense of community.

- **Kilnsey Show (August, Wharfedale)** – One of the most famous shows in the Dales, dating back to 1897. Expect sheepdog trials, horse jumping, local crafts, and even harness racing against the dramatic backdrop of Kilnsey Crag.
- **Reeth Show (August, Swaledale)** – A traditional country show with sheep competitions, stone walling demonstrations, fell races, and children's activities. It feels like stepping back into rural England of decades past.
- **Malham Show (August, near Malham Cove)** – Set in one of the most scenic parts of the Dales, this show features livestock, dry stone walling contests, and classic fell running races up the surrounding hills.

These agricultural shows often end with community dances, brass band performances, or simply neighbors catching up—making them the beating heart of rural Yorkshire life.

2. Traditional Fairs & Folk Events

The Dales also hosts unique fairs and folk gatherings rooted in centuries of tradition. Many of these events showcase quirky local customs that might surprise and delight visitors.

- **Masham Sheep Fair (September, Masham)** – A highlight of the Dales calendar, celebrating the town's long history of sheep trading. Expect parades of sheep through the market square, sheep racing, wool demonstrations, and craft stalls. It's both charming and educational.
- **Grassington Festival (June)** – A mix of art, music, and street performances in the heart of the Dales. This event transforms Grassington into a lively hub with everything from folk music to outdoor theatre.
- **Richmond Meet (Spring Bank Holiday, Richmond)** – A traditional fair with parades, maypole dancing, children's activities, and plenty of community spirit.

3. Seasonal Festivals & Food Celebrations

The Dales' festivals often revolve around the changing seasons and the bounty of the land. These gatherings are not only fun but also deeply tied to the area's farming calendar.

- **Swaledale Festival (late May to early June)** – A two-week celebration of music and the arts held in various venues across Swaledale and Wensleydale. From classical music concerts in historic churches to folk performances in village halls, this festival brings world-class art into intimate settings.
- **Yorkshire Dales Food & Drink Festival (July, Skipton)** – A paradise for food lovers, featuring celebrity chef demos, cooking workshops, artisan food stalls, and live music. It's one of the biggest events in the region and perfect for families.
- **Apple Day (October, various villages)** – A fun seasonal festival where villages celebrate the apple harvest with cider-making demonstrations, apple bobbing, and local produce tastings.

4. Sporting Events & Outdoor Challenges

Given the dramatic landscape of the Dales, it's no surprise that many local events revolve around outdoor sports. From traditional fell running to endurance cycling, these events showcase both the rugged beauty of the land and the resilience of those who take part.

- **Three Peaks Fell Race (April/May)** – A grueling 23-mile race over the peaks of Pen-y-ghent, Ingleborough, and Whernside. Even if you don't participate, it's inspiring to watch.
- **Dales Festival of Food & Drink and Cycling Events (various)** – With the Tour de France passing through Yorkshire in 2014, cycling events have grown in popularity. Visitors may encounter sportive rides and charity events winding through the valleys.
- **Burnsall Feast & Fell Race (August)** – A village tradition combining games, stalls, and a fell race up the surrounding hills. It's a great example of how sports and community go hand-in-hand in the Dales.

5. Christmas Markets & Winter Traditions

The Yorkshire Dales don't slow down in winter. Many villages light up with festive cheer during Christmas markets, carol singing, and seasonal fairs.

- **Grassington Dickensian Festival (December)** – Perhaps the most magical winter event in the Dales. The village transforms into a Dickens-era market with costumed characters, roasted chestnuts, traditional carols, and horse-drawn carriages. It's a step back in time and perfect for families.
- **Kettlewell Christmas Lights** – A small village that goes all out with festive displays, community gatherings, and local stalls.

Practical Tips for Visitors

- **Check Dates Early** – Many events are annual and have fixed dates, but they can change slightly depending on local calendars, so it's worth checking before planning your trip.
- **Book Accommodation in Advance** – Popular festivals like the Kilnsey Show or Grassington Festival attract crowds, so nearby inns and B&Bs fill quickly.
- **Get Involved** – Don't just observe—try local foods, join in traditional dances, or cheer on runners at a fell race. These moments create the most memorable travel experiences.

7. Food & Drink of the Dales

7.1 Traditional Yorkshire Cuisine

The Yorkshire Dales is not just a feast for the eyes—it's also a feast for the stomach. The food here reflects the land itself: hearty, simple, and full of flavor. Rooted in centuries of farming traditions, the local cuisine has been shaped by the rugged hills, fertile valleys, and the hardworking communities that have lived here for generations. Eating in the Dales is more than filling your belly—it's tasting history and culture on a plate.

The Famous Yorkshire Pudding

No dish is more closely tied to Yorkshire than the legendary **Yorkshire pudding**. Originally a simple, baked batter made from flour, eggs, and milk, it was designed to be filling and cheap, stretching out meat portions during Sunday dinners. Today, it's still served with roast beef and gravy, but in Yorkshire, it's also enjoyed in creative ways—filled with sausages, vegetables, or even used as a giant edible bowl.

Hearty Comfort Food for Farmers

The Dales' farming heritage gave rise to **warming, energy-rich meals** that could sustain workers through long days in the fields and hills. Dishes like:

- **Wensleydale Cheese Pie** – combining the region's iconic cheese with potatoes and onions in a golden crust.
- **Yorkshire Curd Tart** – a sweet dessert made with curds, currants, and a hint of nutmeg.
- **Game Stews and Pies** – filled with venison, rabbit, or pheasant from the surrounding moors.

Wensleydale Cheese

Perhaps the most famous product of the Dales, **Wensleydale cheese** has been crafted here since the 12th century, when Cistercian monks first introduced it. With its crumbly texture and fresh, slightly sweet flavor, it's delicious on its own, but also famously paired with fruitcake or apple pie—a quirky Yorkshire tradition that surprises many visitors but delights those who try it.

Bread, Pies & Bakes

Bakeries across the Dales keep alive recipes passed down through generations. You'll find:

- **Fat Rascals** – large fruit scones, often topped with cherries and almonds, perfect with a pot of Yorkshire tea.
- **Parkin** – a sticky ginger cake made with oats and treacle, traditionally eaten around Bonfire Night but enjoyed year-round.
- **Meat & Potato Pies** – a staple of Yorkshire kitchens and pub menus.

Yorkshire Tea Culture

No mention of Yorkshire cuisine would be complete without **Yorkshire tea**. Known as one of the strongest and most beloved brews in the UK, it's often served with milk and sometimes sugar, always alongside biscuits or a slice of cake. In the Dales, afternoon tea can be an event in itself, complete with sandwiches, scones, and cakes served in charming tearooms.

Farm-to-Table Freshness

One of the delights of eating in the Dales is the **freshness of ingredients**. Many pubs and inns proudly use local lamb, beef, and vegetables, with menus that change with the seasons. Farmers' markets in towns like Skipton and Richmond showcase everything from fresh eggs and honey to artisanal cheeses and chutneys, offering visitors the chance to taste the Dales' bounty straight from the source.

In short: Traditional Yorkshire cuisine is honest, hearty, and steeped in heritage. From the iconic Yorkshire pudding to crumbly Wensleydale cheese and rustic pies, food here warms both body and soul, connecting you to the land and the people who have shaped it.

7.2 Local Pubs, Tea Rooms & Farm Shops

One of the greatest joys of exploring the Yorkshire Dales is pausing from the open landscapes and finding comfort in its welcoming pubs, charming tea rooms, and rustic farm shops. These are not just places to eat and drink—they are hubs of local life where tradition meets hospitality.

Pubs: The Heart of the Dales

The Yorkshire pub is legendary, and in the Dales, it often doubles as a slice of living history. Many have stood for centuries, their thick stone walls and low-beamed ceilings offering a warm retreat from the elements.

- **Atmosphere:** Expect roaring fires in winter, friendly chatter at the bar, and often a mix of locals, walkers, and cyclists all sharing space.
- **Food & Drink:** Alongside hand-pulled local ales (look for Black Sheep, Theakston, or Timothy Taylor's), most pubs serve hearty meals such as steak and ale pie, Yorkshire sausages, and Sunday roasts.
- **Examples:**
    - *The Buck Inn* (Malham) – Popular with walkers tackling Malham Cove, known for its hearty portions.
    - *The Kings Arms* (Askrigg) – A historic inn made famous by the TV series *All Creatures Great and Small*.
    - *Tan Hill Inn* – Britain's highest pub at 1,732 feet, offering sweeping views and a truly unique experience.

Tea Rooms: A Yorkshire Institution

No trip to the Dales would be complete without tea and cake in a cozy tea room. Yorkshire is famous for its afternoon teas, with freshly baked scones, clotted cream, and homemade jams.

- **Tradition:** Expect proper pots of tea (often Yorkshire Tea), china cups, and shelves of cakes and traybakes.
- **Specialties:** Don't miss fat rascals (a fruity scone-like treat), parkin (a sticky ginger cake), or a slice of Victoria sponge.
- **Examples:**
    - *The Creamery Tea Room* (Hawes) – Perfect for pairing with a visit to the Wensleydale Creamery.
    - *The Old School Tea Room* (Hebden) – Quirky, rustic, and loved for its homemade cakes.
    - *Betty's Tea Rooms* (Harrogate, not in the Dales but nearby) – An iconic Yorkshire experience if passing through.

Farm Shops: Field-to-Fork Freshness

Farm shops in the Dales connect visitors directly with the land, offering fresh, local produce and handmade goods. These are ideal for stocking up on picnic supplies or taking a taste of Yorkshire home.

- **What to Expect:**
    - Locally reared meats such as Dales lamb, pork pies, and artisan sausages.
    - Cheeses including the famous Wensleydale, often available in unique flavors.
    - Jams, chutneys, honey, and baked goods crafted by small local producers.
- **Examples:**
    - *Berry's Farm Shop & Café* (Swaledale) – Known for its deli counter and scenic café setting.
    - *Keelham Farm Shop* (Skipton) – A treasure trove of Yorkshire produce, from fresh bread .
    - *Town End Farm Shop* (Airton, Malhamdale) – Small but excellent, with an emphasis on sustainable local produce.

Why These Matter

Pubs, tea rooms, and farm shops in the Dales are more than just places to eat—they are experiences in themselves. They give you a chance to slow down, meet locals, and taste the traditions that have shaped life here for centuries. Whether you're warming up after a windswept hike with a pint by the fire, indulging in a cream tea with a view of rolling hills, or browsing shelves of homemade preserves in a farm shop, these moments add flavor and heart to your Yorkshire Dales adventure.

7.3 Food Experiences & Farmers' Markets

The Yorkshire Dales is more than just a feast for the eyes—it's also a haven for food lovers. From bustling farmers' markets brimming with regional specialties to immersive experiences where visitors can meet producers, taste fresh flavors, and learn traditional skills, food in the Dales is about connection: to the land, to the people, and to centuries of culinary tradition.

Farmers' Markets: Local Flavor at Its Best

Farmers' markets across the Dales showcase the region's vibrant food culture. These markets are filled with stalls offering artisanal cheeses, fresh-baked breads, organic meats, homemade chutneys, and seasonal produce. Popular markets include:

- **Richmond Farmers' Market** (third Saturday of the month) – A lively market held in the cobbled Georgian marketplace, featuring award-winning cheeses, pies, and preserves.
- **Skipton Farmers' Market** – Known for its variety, with local butchers, fishmongers, and bakers standing alongside producers of Yorkshire chutneys and pickles.
- **Leyburn Farmers' Market** – A smaller but authentic gathering where visitors can meet local farmers selling lamb, honey, and Dales cheeses.

These markets not only provide fresh produce but also give travelers a chance to talk directly with the people who grow, farm, and create the food.

Hands-On Food Experiences

The Dales also offers experiences for those who want to go beyond tasting:

- **Cheese-Making Workshops** – Wensleydale Creamery in Hawes runs tours and workshops where visitors can watch traditional cheese-making demonstrations and even try crafting their own.
- **Foraging Walks** – Guided foraging tours in the Dales teach participants how to identify edible wild plants, mushrooms, and herbs, offering a new appreciation of the land's natural bounty.
- **Cookery Schools** – Rural cookery schools, such as those near Skipton, often feature courses on Yorkshire baking, game cookery, and traditional Dales recipes.

Seasonal Food Festivals

Several festivals bring together the best of the Dales' food culture:

- **Leyburn Food Festival** – A celebration of Yorkshire produce, with street food, cooking demonstrations, and live music.
- **Malham Show & Kilnsey Show** – Agricultural shows that combine traditional competitions with hearty food stalls, showcasing the best lamb, beef, and baking from the region.
- **Settle Stories' Food & Drink Events** – Blending storytelling with food experiences, offering a unique way to enjoy Dales culture.

Why It Matters

These food experiences and markets highlight the Dales' dedication to sustainable farming, community spirit, and preserving culinary traditions. Whether it's tasting a crumbly slice of Wensleydale cheese, sipping locally brewed cider, or buying fresh rhubarb straight from the grower, every bite tells a story of Yorkshire's land and heritage.

7.3 Food Experiences & Farmers' Markets

The Yorkshire Dales is more than just a feast for the eyes—it's also a haven for food lovers. From bustling farmers' markets brimming with regional specialties to immersive experiences where visitors can meet producers, taste fresh flavors, and learn traditional skills, food in the Dales is about connection: to the land, to the people, and to centuries of culinary tradition.

Farmers' Markets: Local Flavor at Its Best

Farmers' markets across the Dales showcase the region's vibrant food culture. These markets are filled with stalls offering artisanal cheeses, fresh-baked breads, organic meats, homemade chutneys, and seasonal produce. Popular markets include:

- **Richmond Farmers' Market** (third Saturday of the month) – A lively market held in the cobbled Georgian marketplace, featuring award-winning cheeses, pies, and preserves.
- **Skipton Farmers' Market** – Known for its variety, with local butchers, fishmongers, and bakers standing alongside producers of Yorkshire chutneys and pickles.
- **Leyburn Farmers' Market** – A smaller but authentic gathering where visitors can meet local farmers selling lamb, honey, and Dales cheeses.

These markets not only provide fresh produce but also give travelers a chance to talk directly with the people who grow, farm, and create the food.

Hands-On Food Experiences

The Dales also offers experiences for those who want to go beyond tasting:

- **Cheese-Making Workshops** – Wensleydale Creamery in Hawes runs tours and workshops where visitors can watch traditional cheese-making demonstrations and even try crafting their own.
- **Foraging Walks** – Guided foraging tours in the Dales teach participants how to identify edible wild plants, mushrooms, and herbs, offering a new appreciation of the land's natural bounty.
- **Cookery Schools** – Rural cookery schools, such as those near Skipton, often feature courses on Yorkshire baking, game cookery, and traditional Dales recipes.

Seasonal Food Festivals

Several festivals bring together the best of the Dales' food culture:

- **Leyburn Food Festival** – A celebration of Yorkshire produce, with street food, cooking demonstrations, and live music.
- **Malham Show & Kilnsey Show** – Agricultural shows that combine traditional competitions with hearty food stalls, showcasing the best lamb, beef, and baking from the region.
- **Settle Stories' Food & Drink Events** – Blending storytelling with food experiences, offering a unique way to enjoy Dales culture.

Why It Matters

These food experiences and markets highlight the Dales' dedication to sustainable farming, community spirit, and preserving culinary traditions. Whether it's tasting a crumbly slice of Wensleydale cheese, sipping locally brewed cider, or buying fresh rhubarb straight from the grower, every bite tells a story of Yorkshire's land and heritage.

8. Where to Stay in the Yorkshire Dales

8.1 Cozy Cottages, B&Bs & Inns

One of the joys of visiting the Yorkshire Dales is waking up in a charming stone cottage, a centuries-old inn, or a family-run B&B that feels like home. These accommodations capture the essence of the Dales—warm hospitality, rustic charm, and a chance to live like a local while surrounded by breathtaking scenery.

1. Cozy Cottages

Renting a cottage is perfect for those who want privacy, flexibility, and a "home away from home" feel. Many are traditional stone-built houses with roaring fireplaces, low-beamed ceilings, and views of rolling hills or village greens.

- **Who it's for:** Families, couples, or groups who enjoy self-catering and want to set their own pace.
- **Features:** Fully equipped kitchens, outdoor gardens, wood-burning stoves, and sometimes pet-friendly options.
- **Best Villages for Cottages:**
    - **Grassington** – Ideal for walkers with shops and pubs nearby.

- - **Reeth in Swaledale** – Surrounded by valleys and meadows, great for peace and quiet.
  - **Aysgarth & Hawes** – Close to waterfalls, cheese dairies, and local attractions.
- **Tip:** Book early for summer and Christmas, as cottages are highly sought-after for holiday stays.

2. Bed & Breakfasts (B&Bs)

B&Bs are a Yorkshire Dales tradition—friendly hosts, hearty breakfasts, and plenty of local tips. They're often family-run, which means you'll get personal recommendations on walks, pubs, and hidden gems.

- **Who it's for:** Solo travelers, couples, or anyone who enjoys personal hospitality.
- **Features:** Comfortable bedrooms, full English breakfasts with local produce (think Dales sausages, eggs, and black pudding), and warm conversation with hosts.
- **Popular Locations for B&Bs:**
  - **Skipton** – The gateway to the Dales, with easy access to attractions.
  - **Hawes** – Famous for Wensleydale cheese and good for walkers.
  - **Malham** – Perfect if you want to stay close to Malham Cove and Gordale Scar.
- **Tip:** Many B&Bs are in old farmhouses, so expect creaky floors and quirky layouts—they add to the charm.

3. Historic Inns & Country Pubs

The Dales are dotted with centuries-old coaching inns and traditional pubs where you can stay overnight. These combine rustic comfort with character, often offering hearty pub meals and a pint by the fire after a long day outdoors.

- **Who it's for:** Walkers and cyclists who want food, drink, and lodging all under one roof.
- **Features:** Wooden beams, log fires, traditional ales, Yorkshire puddings, and cozy bedrooms upstairs.
- **Famous Inns:**
  - **The Black Swan, Ravenstonedale** – Known for fine food and character.
  - **The Buck Inn, Malham** – A walker's favorite near Malham Cove.
  - **The King's Arms, Askrigg** – Once used as a filming location for *All Creatures Great and Small*.

- **Tip:** Many pubs double as community hubs, so staying here gives you a real taste of village life.

4. What to Expect

- **Atmosphere:** Relaxed, welcoming, with a slower pace of life.
- **Budget:** Prices vary—cottages are usually more expensive (especially in peak season), while B&Bs and inns can be budget-friendly.
- **Meals:** Cottages are self-catering; B&Bs usually include breakfast; inns provide full meals with plenty of Yorkshire specialties.
- **Booking:** Always book well ahead in summer, bank holidays, and Christmas.

Insider Tip: If you want the best of both worlds, stay in a cottage for a week-long base and book one or two nights in a historic inn during your trip. This way you'll experience both independence and local hospitality.

8.2 Family-Friendly Stays & Camping

The Yorkshire Dales is an excellent choice for families, offering accommodation that blends comfort, convenience, and the chance to immerse yourself in the outdoors. Whether you're after a campsite under the stars, a holiday park packed with activities, or a cozy family-run B&B, there are plenty of options designed with families in mind.

Family-Friendly Hotels & Holiday Parks

- **Holiday Parks & Lodges** – Places like **Riverside Caravan Park** in Ingleton and **Vale of Pickering Caravan Park** are popular with families. They provide playgrounds, safe open spaces, and sometimes even swimming pools or organized activities, making them ideal for children to play while parents relax.
- **Farm Stays** – A stay on a working farm, such as **Howgill Lodge near Appletreewick**, gives kids a hands-on countryside experience. Many farms allow children to meet animals, collect eggs, or explore the land safely.
- **Family-Run B&Bs** – Many smaller inns and guesthouses across the Dales cater to families with spacious rooms, highchairs, and warm hospitality, often giving you that "home away from home" feel.

Camping & Glamping

For families who love the outdoors, camping in the Yorkshire Dales is a memorable way to experience nature:

- **Traditional Camping** – Campsites like **Wharfedale Camping & Caravanning Club Site** and **Hawes Caravan & Motorhome Club Site** offer excellent facilities including shower blocks, laundry, and playgrounds. These sites are well-maintained, safe, and close to walking and cycling trails.
- **Glamping Pods & Safari Tents** – For families wanting the adventure of camping without giving up comfort, glamping is the answer. Many sites now offer heated wooden pods, yurts, or safari tents complete with real beds, lighting, and even Wi-Fi. This option is especially great for families with younger kids who may not be ready for full camping.
- **Wild Camping** (with caution) – Though not generally permitted in the Dales without landowner permission, some families choose more adventurous wild camping with older children. Always follow local rules, leave no trace, and camp responsibly.

Tips for Families Staying in the Dales

- **Book Early** – Family-friendly accommodations, especially during school holidays, book up quickly.
- **Check Facilities** – Look for campsites or stays with essentials like child-safe areas, family bathrooms, and indoor playrooms in case of rainy weather.
- **Bring Layers** – Even in summer, evenings in the Dales can get chilly, so bring warm clothes and extra bedding for little ones.
- **Mix & Match** – Consider splitting your trip: a few nights in a cottage for comfort, followed by camping or glamping for the adventure.

From roasting marshmallows by the campfire to waking up to sheep grazing outside your tent, family-friendly stays in the Yorkshire Dales make your trip both comfortable and exciting—leaving children with lifelong countryside memories.

8.3 Luxury Retreats & Unique Accommodations

While the Yorkshire Dales are best known for their stone cottages and rustic farmhouses, the region also offers a surprising number of **luxury retreats and unique stays**. These options combine comfort, character, and the charm of the Dales' natural surroundings. Whether you're after a spa getaway, a boutique hotel with sweeping views, or an unusual stay like a shepherd's hut or converted castle, there's something here for every taste.

Luxury Country Hotels & Spa Retreats

For travelers who want a mix of classic elegance and modern comfort, the Dales' luxury country hotels provide fine dining, spacious suites, landscaped gardens, and wellness experiences.

- **Yorebridge House (Bainbridge, Wensleydale)**
  A 5-star boutique hotel in a former Victorian schoolhouse. Some rooms have **private outdoor hot tubs** with valley views. The on-site restaurant serves award-winning fine dining.

  - **Cost:** £250–£400 per night
  - **Best for:** Romantic getaways, special occasions

- **The Devonshire Arms Hotel & Spa (Bolton Abbey, Wharfedale)**
  A luxury hotel on the Duke of Devonshire's estate with **Michelin-starred dining**, spa treatments, and countryside walks right from the doorstep.

  - **Cost:** £280–£450 per night
  - **Best for:** Luxury seekers, spa breaks, food lovers

- **The Coniston Hotel & Spa (near Skipton)**
  Set on a large estate with a lake, this hotel offers outdoor activities (archery, fishing, off-road driving) alongside a **state-of-the-art spa** with outdoor infinity pools.

  - **Cost:** £200–£350 per night
  - **Best for:** Couples, spa weekends, active luxury

Boutique & Stylish Stays

For those who prefer intimate charm with modern style, boutique accommodations in the Dales often blend historic architecture with chic interiors.

- **The Traddock (Austwick, near Ingleton)**
  A Georgian country house with individually designed rooms and a focus on **local Yorkshire produce** in its fine dining restaurant.

  - **Cost:** £180–£280 per night
  - **Best for:** Couples, foodies, slow travel

- **The Black Swan (Ravenstonedale, edge of the Dales)**
  A stylish inn with a balance of rustic character and modern touches, offering gourmet dining and beautifully furnished rooms.

  - **Cost:** £150–£220 per night
  - **Best for:** Couples, those wanting boutique charm

Castles, Halls & Historic Estates

For a stay that feels truly special, you can spend the night in a **castle, hall, or historic estate**, many of which have been converted into luxurious hotels or guesthouses.

- **Swinton Park Castle Hotel (Masham, Nidderdale)**
  A 17th-century castle turned luxury hotel, complete with **opulent suites, walled gardens, a spa, and cookery school**.

  - **Cost:** £250–£500 per night
  - **Best for:** History lovers, families wanting a grand experience
- **Hazlewood Castle (Tadcaster, just outside the Dales)**
  A medieval castle with four-poster beds and grounds for outdoor activities like archery and falconry.

  - **Cost:** £200–£350 per night
  - **Best for:** Weddings, celebrations, heritage enthusiasts

Unique & Quirky Stays

If you'd like something different, the Dales also offer **glamping pods, shepherd's huts, treehouses, and converted barns**, letting you combine nature with comfort.

- **Littondale Country & Leisure Park (Arncliffe, Littondale)**
  Luxury glamping pods with heating, en-suite bathrooms, and stunning views of the valley.

  - **Cost:** £90–£150 per night
  - **Best for:** Families, couples, budget-friendly luxury
- **Keld Lodge Shepherd's Huts (Swaledale)**
  Cosy, hand-built huts with wood-burning stoves and peaceful riverside settings.

  - **Cost:** £100–£140 per night
  - **Best for:** Couples seeking seclusion
- **Treehouses at Swinton Bivouac (Masham)**
  Rustic yet stylish treehouses with log-burning stoves and woodland views. A unique choice for families or small groups.

  - **Cost:** £150–£250 per night
  - **Best for:** Families, adventurous travelers

Luxury Self-Catering Barns & Lodges

For more independence while keeping the luxury, you can stay in **converted barns, lodges, or designer cottages** with hot tubs, open fires, and countryside views.

- **Dalesend Cottages (Bedale, on the Dales' edge)**
  Four stylish cottages with **private hot tubs, chic interiors, and open-plan living**.

  - **Cost:** £180–£300 per night
  - **Best for:** Couples, long stays
- **Broughton Hall Estate (near Skipton)**
  A historic estate offering luxury lodges, eco-retreats, and country houses for private rental.

  - **Cost:** £250–£600 per night depending on property size
  - **Best for:** Groups, wellness retreats, celebrations

Tip for Travelers:
Luxury accommodations in the Yorkshire Dales are very popular during **summer (June–August)** and **autumn weekends** when the foliage is spectacular. For the best deals, book midweek or during the **spring (April–May)** when wildflowers cover the hillsides.

9. Suggested Itineraries

9.1 2-Day Highlights of the Dales

If you only have two days in the Yorkshire Dales, you'll want to make the most of your time by blending scenic landscapes, charming villages, and cultural experiences. This short itinerary gives you a real flavor of the region—without feeling rushed.

Day 1: Southern Dales – Villages, Waterfalls & History

Morning – Skipton & Bolton Abbey

- Begin in **Skipton**, the "Gateway to the Dales." Visit **Skipton Castle** (entry around £10), one of the best-preserved medieval castles in England. Wander through Skipton's lively market (held most days except Sunday) to browse local produce and crafts.
- Drive (15 minutes) to **Bolton Abbey**, where you can explore the romantic priory ruins and walk along the River Wharfe. The riverside paths are family-friendly, with highlights like the **stepping stones** across the river. Parking ~£15 per car for the day.

Afternoon – Grassington & Linton Falls

- Head to **Grassington**, a traditional market town with cobbled streets, artisan shops, and friendly pubs. Have lunch at a cozy inn like **The Devonshire Grassington** (mains £12–£18).
- Stroll to **Linton Falls**, a short, scenic walk where the River Wharfe tumbles dramatically over rocks. Perfect for photography.

Late Afternoon – Malham & Gordale Scar

- Continue to **Malham**, one of the Dales' most iconic spots.
    - Visit **Malham Cove**, a huge limestone cliff with a unique pavement at the top.
    - Nearby, **Gordale Scar** is a dramatic gorge with waterfalls hidden within.
- Walking here is relatively easy but can be rocky, so wear sturdy shoes.

Evening – Stay Overnight in Malham or Grassington

- **Budget option:** B&B in Grassington (£70–£100 per night).
- **Mid-range option: Beck Hall Malham**, a dog-friendly riverside inn (rooms £110–£150).

- **Luxury: The Devonshire Arms Hotel & Spa, Bolton Abbey** (rooms from £180).

Enjoy a pub dinner—try a hearty Yorkshire pie with local ale.

Day 2: Northern Dales – Valleys, Villages & Views

Morning – Wensleydale & Aysgarth Falls

- Drive north to **Aysgarth Falls**, famous for their beauty and their appearance in *Robin Hood: Prince of Thieves*. Easy riverside walks connect the upper, middle, and lower falls. Parking ~£5.
- Visit the **Wensleydale Creamery in Hawes** (£5.50 entry), where you can taste the famous cheese, watch demonstrations, and enjoy a light breakfast or coffee.

Afternoon – Hawes, Hardraw & Buttertubs Pass

- Explore **Hawes**, a lively market town with antique shops, tearooms, and the **Dales Countryside Museum** (entry £6).
- Walk to **Hardraw Force**, England's highest single-drop waterfall (entry £5 via the Green Dragon Inn).
- Take a scenic drive over **Buttertubs Pass**, a high mountain road with stunning views of the valleys below—one of the most dramatic drives in England.

Late Afternoon – Swaledale & Reeth

- Continue to **Swaledale**, a valley of wildflower meadows, stone barns, and dry-stone walls.
- Stop in **Reeth**, a postcard-pretty village with a large green, perfect for a stroll and afternoon tea. Try the **Reeth Ice Cream Parlour** or a pint at **The Buck Hotel**.

Evening – Return or Overnight

- If heading back, you can loop toward **Richmond**, with its castle ruins and Georgian architecture.
- Overnight options:
    - **Budget:** Local B&B in Hawes (~£75).
    - **Mid-range: Stone House Hotel, Hawes** (£130–£170).
    - **Luxury: Yorebridge House, Bainbridge** (boutique hotel with hot tubs, rooms from £220).

Dinner suggestion: Treat yourself at **Yorebridge House Restaurant** (fine dining, tasting menus from £65) or enjoy traditional pub fare in Reeth or Hawes.

This 2-day itinerary balances history, culture, villages, waterfalls, and dramatic scenery—a perfect introduction for first-time visitors to the Yorkshire Dales.

9.2 4–5 Day Journey Through Villages & Landscapes

For travelers who want a deeper immersion into the Yorkshire Dales, a **4–5 day journey** allows you to explore the region's picturesque villages, breathtaking valleys, historic landmarks, and natural wonders at a comfortable pace. This itinerary blends culture, adventure, and relaxation, offering a full experience of the Dales' charm.

Day 1: Southern Dales – Skipton & Grassington

Morning – Skipton

- Begin in **Skipton**, the "Gateway to the Dales," and visit **Skipton Castle**, a well-preserved medieval fortress. Wander along the cobbled High Street, stopping at artisan shops and local cafes.
- Consider a gentle stroll along the **Leeds-Liverpool Canal**, perfect for family-friendly walking and cycling.

Afternoon – Grassington

- Drive to **Grassington**, a charming market town with cobbled streets and historic buildings.
- Lunch at a traditional inn or café featuring **local Yorkshire cuisine**.
- Explore the nearby **Linton Falls**, an easy walking trail with cascading waterfalls ideal for photos.

Evening – Stay Overnight

- Accommodation options:
    - B&Bs: £70–£100 per night
    - Mid-range inns: £110–£150 per night
    - Luxury: **Devonshire Arms, Grassington** (£180+)

Day 2: Malham & Northern Limestone Landscapes

Morning – Malham Cove & Gordale Scar

- Visit **Malham Cove**, a dramatic limestone amphitheater with a flat walk to the top offering panoramic views.
- Continue to **Gordale Scar**, a stunning gorge with waterfalls and unique rock formations.

Afternoon – Janet's Foss & Local Walks

- Stop at **Janet's Foss**, a small but enchanting waterfall and woodland area near Malham.
- Take shorter walks around Malham village or explore the limestone pavements for geology enthusiasts.

Evening – Stay in Malham or nearby Reeth

- B&B: £70–£120 per night
- Cottage rental: £120–£250 per night

Day 3: Wensleydale & Waterfall Exploration

Morning – Aysgarth Falls

- Drive to **Aysgarth Falls**, a series of wide, cascading waterfalls with well-maintained riverside paths.
- Walk the upper, middle, and lower falls for a full experience.

Afternoon – Hawes & Wensleydale Creamery

- Visit **Hawes**, a lively market town, and enjoy lunch in a local café.
- Explore the **Wensleydale Creamery** for cheese-making demonstrations and tastings.

Optional Evening – Buttertubs Pass Drive

- Take a scenic drive through **Buttertubs Pass**, a dramatic high road with panoramic views over valleys and hills.
- Overnight in Hawes or nearby villages (B&B £80–£120, luxury hotel £220+).

Day 4: Swaledale & Hidden Villages

Morning – Reeth & Arkengarthdale

- Explore **Reeth**, a picturesque village with cafes, galleries, and traditional architecture.
- Walk along **Swaledale's trails**, including routes to Arkengarthdale, a valley with wildflowers, stone barns, and rolling hills.

Afternoon – Muker & Keld

- Continue north to **Muker**, a tranquil village with beautiful walking paths.
- Visit **Keld**, known for historic packhorse bridges and unspoiled scenery.
- Optional short hike along the **Pennine Way** for adventurous travelers.

Evening – Overnight Stay

- B&B or small inn in Reeth or Muker (£80–£150)
- Cottage or lodge for groups (£120–£300)

Day 5: Northern Peaks & Scenic Finale

Morning – Ingleborough or Pen-y-Ghent Hike

- For hikers, take a morning trek up **Ingleborough** or **Pen-y-Ghent**, two of the famous Yorkshire Three Peaks. These offer breathtaking views over the Dales.
- Non-hikers can explore **Ribblehead Viaduct**, an engineering marvel with dramatic surroundings.

Afternoon – Settle & Return Journey

- Stop at **Settle**, a market town known for its historic railway station and local shops.
- Enjoy a farewell lunch at a traditional pub or café.

Evening – Departure or Additional Overnight

- Return to your base or stay overnight in **Settle or Skipton** depending on your travel schedule.

Tips for a 4–5 Day Dales Journey

1. **Travel Pace:** Spread hikes and sightseeing over several days to fully enjoy the scenery without rushing.
2. **Accommodation:** Mix B&Bs, cottages, and boutique stays for variety. Booking ahead is essential during peak season.

3. **Transport:** A car is recommended for maximum flexibility, especially for reaching remote villages. Public transport is possible but limited in frequency.
4. **Weather Preparedness:** Bring waterproofs and sturdy walking shoes—even in summer, the weather can change quickly.
5. **Food & Refreshments:** Plan meals around local cafés, pubs, and creamery visits to experience authentic Yorkshire cuisine.

This **4–5 day itinerary** balances walking, driving, village exploration, waterfalls, and scenic highlights, giving travelers a deep and memorable experience of the Yorkshire Dales.

9.3 A Full Week in the Dales: History, Hiking & Hidden Gems

Spending a full week in the Yorkshire Dales allows you to immerse yourself fully in its **stunning landscapes, charming villages, historic sites, and outdoor adventures**. This itinerary combines scenic walks, hidden gems, cultural experiences, and local cuisine, giving travelers a rich, unhurried journey through the heart of the Dales.

Day 1: Arrival & Southern Dales Introduction

Morning – Skipton & Canal Walks

- Begin your trip in **Skipton**, the "Gateway to the Dales."
- Explore **Skipton Castle**, a remarkably preserved medieval fortress.
- Stroll along the **Leeds-Liverpool Canal**, enjoying the scenic towpaths, locks, and wildlife along the way.

Afternoon – Grassington & Linton Falls

- Drive to **Grassington**, a historic market town with cobbled streets and boutique shops.
- Walk to **Linton Falls**, an easily accessible waterfall surrounded by limestone cliffs.
- Enjoy lunch at a café or pub in Grassington.

Evening – Overnight Stay

- Suggested: B&B (£80–£120), mid-range inn (£130–£180), or luxury stay (**Devonshire Arms Hotel & Spa**, £180+).

Day 2: Malham & Limestone Landscapes

Morning – Malham Cove

- Explore **Malham Cove**, a limestone amphitheater formed by glaciers. Walk the trail to the top for panoramic views.

Afternoon – Gordale Scar & Janet's Foss

- Continue to **Gordale Scar**, a dramatic gorge with waterfalls tucked between towering cliffs.
- Visit **Janet's Foss**, a small waterfall in a woodland setting, ideal for a gentle stroll or picnic.

Evening – Stay Overnight in Malham or nearby Reeth

- Accommodation: B&B or cottage rental (£70–£250 per night).

Day 3: Wensleydale & Waterfall Wonders

Morning – Aysgarth Falls

- Walk the riverside trails of **Aysgarth Falls**, a sequence of three wide, cascading waterfalls surrounded by meadows.

Afternoon – Hawes & Wensleydale Creamery

- Explore **Hawes**, a market town with charming streets and artisan shops.
- Visit the **Wensleydale Creamery** for cheese-making demonstrations and tastings.

Evening – Optional Buttertubs Pass Drive

- Take the scenic **Buttertubs Pass**, a high moorland road with breathtaking views over the valleys.
- Overnight in Hawes or nearby villages (B&B £80–£120, mid-range hotel £150–£220).

Day 4: Swaledale & Hidden Villages

Morning – Reeth & Arkengarthdale

- Explore **Reeth**, a quintessential village with galleries, tea rooms, and historic buildings.

- Walk into **Arkengarthdale**, a quiet valley with wildflowers, dry-stone walls, and traditional barns.

Afternoon – Muker & Keld

- Visit **Muker**, a tranquil village with riverside walks and charming cottages.
- Continue to **Keld**, where historic packhorse bridges and streams create postcard-perfect scenery.
- Optional hike: a short section of the **Pennine Way**.

Evening – Overnight Stay

- Accommodation: local B&B (£80–£150), small inns, or self-catering cottages.

Day 5: Northern Peaks & Scenic Engineering

Morning – Ingleborough or Pen-y-Ghent Hike

- Take a hike up **Ingleborough** (10 km round trip) or **Pen-y-Ghent** for panoramic views of the Dales.
- Non-hikers: explore the **Ribblehead Viaduct**, a Victorian engineering marvel with stunning surrounding landscapes.

Afternoon – Settle

- Visit **Settle**, a market town with historic buildings and boutique shops.
- Optional: take the **Settle-Carlisle Railway** scenic ride (one of England's most famous heritage railways).

Evening – Overnight in Settle or nearby

- Suggested accommodation: boutique hotels or cottages (£100–£250).

Day 6: Upper Dales & Castles

Morning – Bolton Castle

- Drive to **Bolton Castle**, a well-preserved medieval fortress. Take a guided tour and explore the castle grounds.

Afternoon – Leyburn & Local Walks

- Visit **Leyburn**, a charming market town with galleries, cafes, and local shops.
- Optional walk along the **River Ure** or countryside paths.

Evening – Overnight Stay

- Accommodation: charming B&Bs (£80–£150) or luxury boutique hotels (£200+).

Day 7: Hidden Gems & Farewell

Morning – Nidderdale & Pateley Bridge

- Explore **Nidderdale**, an Area of Outstanding Natural Beauty (AONB) with rolling hills and riverside trails.
- Stop at **Pateley Bridge**, a historic village with quaint shops and the **Gouthwaite Reservoir** for a gentle walk.

Afternoon – Relaxation & Departure

- Choose a final walk, photography session, or riverside picnic.
- Head back to Skipton, Harrogate, or your departure point.

Tips for a Full Week in the Dales

1. **Travel Flexibility:** A car is highly recommended for reaching remote villages, waterfalls, and hidden trails.
2. **Mix of Activities:** Alternate between walking, sightseeing, and relaxation to avoid fatigue.
3. **Accommodation Variety:** Combine B&Bs, boutique hotels, luxury stays, and cottages to experience both comfort and rural charm.
4. **Weather Preparedness:** Even in summer, the Dales can be unpredictable. Waterproof jackets, sturdy walking shoes, and layers are essential.
5. **Local Dining:** Try pubs, cafes, creamery tastings, and farm-to-table restaurants for authentic Yorkshire food.
6. **Hidden Gems:** Don't miss lesser-known villages like Keld, Muker, and Arkengarthdale for quiet landscapes away from tourist crowds.

This **7-day itinerary** allows travelers to fully experience the Yorkshire Dales, balancing iconic sights, scenic hikes, cultural heritage, and tranquil villages. By the end of the week, visitors will have a deep connection to both the natural beauty and the rich history of the region.

10. Practical Travel Tips & Resources

10.1 Safety, Weather & Outdoor Preparedness

The Yorkshire Dales is a breathtaking region of rolling hills, limestone valleys, waterfalls, and historic villages. While it is incredibly rewarding to explore, being prepared for **weather changes, terrain, and outdoor safety** is essential for a smooth and enjoyable trip. This section provides detailed guidance for travelers of all levels—from casual walkers to seasoned hikers.

Weather in the Dales

The weather in the Yorkshire Dales can be **unpredictable**, even in summer. Rain, fog, and wind can appear suddenly, especially in the higher falls and remote areas. Understanding seasonal patterns and preparing accordingly will help you enjoy your trip safely.

- **Spring (March–May):** Mild temperatures (10–15°C / 50–59°F) and blooming wildflowers. Occasional showers, so waterproofs are essential. Paths may be muddy after rain.
- **Summer (June–August):** Warmest months (15–22°C / 59–72°F). Long daylight hours make it ideal for hikes and village exploration. Popular spots can be busy, so plan ahead. Afternoon showers are common.
- **Autumn (September–November):** Cooler temperatures (8–15°C / 46–59°F) with crisp air and stunning fall foliage. Early snow is possible in late autumn at higher elevations. Paths can be slippery from fallen leaves.
- **Winter (December–February):** Cold (0–7°C / 32–45°F), with occasional snow or ice. Many remote trails are challenging, and some accommodations may close. Short daylight hours require careful planning for walks.

Tip: Always check the **Met Office Yorkshire Dales forecast** or local visitor centers for up-to-date weather conditions before heading out.

Outdoor Safety

The Dales' natural beauty comes with its own risks, particularly for walkers, hikers, and outdoor adventurers. Safety should always be a priority.

- **Terrain Awareness:**
    - Many trails involve uneven ground, rocky paths, or steep climbs.

- Limestone pavements and waterfall areas can be slippery, especially after rain.
- Always wear **sturdy, waterproof footwear** with good grip.
- **Navigation:**
  - Maps and guidebooks are essential. OS Explorer maps (OL2 & OL30) cover most of the Dales.
  - While mobile GPS can help, **signals may be weak in remote valleys**. Bring a compass and know basic map-reading skills.
- **Walking Safety Tips:**
  - Inform someone of your planned route and expected return time.
  - Stick to marked paths wherever possible; some farmland is private or protected.
  - Carry **water, snacks, and a basic first-aid kit**.
  - Be cautious near rivers, waterfalls, and cliffs.
- **Animal Awareness:**
  - Sheep and cows are common in fields and along paths. Keep dogs on leads near livestock.
  - Some sheepdogs may be protective of their flocks—do not approach.

Clothing & Gear Essentials

The right clothing and gear can make a huge difference in comfort and safety:

- **Waterproof Jacket & Trousers:** Lightweight, breathable, and fully waterproof.
- **Layered Clothing:** Base layers, fleece or wool mid-layers, and windproof outer layers.
- **Footwear:** Waterproof hiking boots with ankle support and strong soles.
- **Hat & Gloves:** Especially important in spring and autumn, when weather can change rapidly.
- **Daypack Essentials:** Map, compass, snacks, water, first-aid kit, mobile phone (fully charged), and a small torch or headlamp.
- **Optional Gear:** Walking poles for steep terrain, binoculars for wildlife spotting, and camera for landscapes.

Emergency Services & Contacts

Knowing how to get help is crucial if anything goes wrong:

- **Emergency Number (UK-wide):** 999 or 112
- **Mountain Rescue (Yorkshire Dales):**
    - **Upper Wharfedale & Malhamdale:** 01756 749 409
    - **Swaledale & Arkengarthdale:** 01748 884 575
    - **Ribblesdale & Ingleborough:** 01729 822 118
- **Local Visitor Centers:** Often provide weather updates, trail information, and safety advice.

Seasonal Considerations

- **Spring & Summer:** Great for wildflowers, walking, cycling, and river activities. Busy periods require early starts for popular trails like Malham Cove.
- **Autumn:** Best for photography, fewer crowds, and wildlife spotting. Carry extra layers as mornings and evenings are cool.
- **Winter:** Only suitable for experienced walkers due to snow, ice, and shorter daylight hours. Check accommodation and road access in advance.

Tips for Outdoor Preparedness

1. **Plan Routes in Advance:** Know the distance, elevation, and difficulty level of each hike or walk.
2. **Check Weather Forecasts:** Mountain weather can change quickly; adapt plans as needed.
3. **Stay Hydrated & Energized:** Carry water and high-energy snacks.
4. **Inform Others of Your Plans:** Especially if exploring remote areas.
5. **Respect the Countryside:** Follow the **Countryside Code**: leave gates as you find them, take litter home, and avoid disturbing wildlife.

By taking **weather precautions, using proper gear, and planning carefully**, exploring the Yorkshire Dales becomes a safe and unforgettable experience. Prepared travelers can fully enjoy the breathtaking landscapes, cascading waterfalls, charming villages, and hidden gems that make the region so special.

10.2 Communication & Connectivity in Rural Areas

While the Yorkshire Dales is renowned for its **tranquil landscapes, rolling hills, and charming villages**, travelers should be aware that rural areas often come with **limited mobile signal, sporadic internet access, and patchy Wi-Fi coverage**. Planning ahead for communication is essential, whether for navigation, emergencies, or simply staying in touch with friends and family.

Mobile Coverage in the Dales

Mobile signal strength varies widely depending on **location, network provider, and terrain**:

- **Towns & Larger Villages:** Skipton, Settle, Hawes, and Richmond generally have **good 4G coverage**, with most providers offering stable voice and data connections.
- **Smaller Villages & Remote Valleys:** Locations such as Muker, Keld, or parts of Swaledale may have **weak or no signal**. Network drops are common near steep hills, moors, and dense valleys.
- **High Peaks & Trails:** Walking routes up Ingleborough, Pen-y-Ghent, or along the Pennine Way often **fall outside mobile coverage**, so do not rely solely on mobile phones for navigation or emergencies.

Tip: Check your network provider's coverage map before traveling. Popular UK providers include EE, Vodafone, O2, and Three, but coverage quality varies in remote areas.

Wi-Fi Availability

- **Hotels, B&Bs & Inns:** Most accommodation offers Wi-Fi, but speeds may be slower in more remote properties. Always confirm access if you plan to work remotely.
- **Cafes & Restaurants:** Larger towns like Skipton, Hawes, and Grassington have Wi-Fi-friendly cafes and pubs. Expect minimal service in smaller villages.
- **Visitor Centers & Libraries:** Some offer free Wi-Fi for tourists and can be a good spot to check emails, weather updates, or travel plans.

Internet & Data Tips for Remote Travel

1. **Offline Maps & Apps:**

    - Download maps on Google Maps, Maps.me, or Ordnance Survey apps in advance.
    - Offline hiking or walking trail apps, like **OS Maps or ViewRanger**, are highly recommended.

2. **Emergency Access:**

    - Keep a **charged mobile phone and power bank** at all times.
    - In areas with no signal, identify **local landmarks or refuges** to reach in case of emergency.

3. **SIM Cards & Roaming:**
    - Visitors from abroad may consider purchasing a **UK SIM card** for better coverage.
    - Be aware that roaming services in remote areas may be unreliable.
4. **Satellite Communication (Optional):**
    - For serious hikers or walkers exploring remote peaks, consider a **satellite messenger device** or GPS tracker for emergencies.

Communication Etiquette in Rural Areas

- Be mindful that **local communities often appreciate quiet and respectful behavior**, especially in small villages and farm areas.
- When using mobile phones in pubs, cafes, or shops, maintain a low volume and avoid blocking walkways.

Practical Communication Tips for Travelers

- **Plan ahead:** Always have printed or downloaded maps, emergency contacts, and directions.
- **Inform someone of your plans:** Especially if hiking or exploring remote trails.
- **Know local resources:** Visitor centers, local inns, and police stations can provide guidance if you lose connectivity.
- **Backup navigation:** Consider a paper map as a failsafe—especially for multi-day hikes or driving across valleys.

By understanding **signal limitations, Wi-Fi availability, and offline tools**, travelers can enjoy the Yorkshire Dales confidently. Even in areas where connectivity is limited, being prepared ensures safety, convenience, and the freedom to fully experience the region's **tranquil beauty and remote landscapes**.

10.3 Final Thoughts & Inspiring Itineraries

As your journey through the Yorkshire Dales comes together, it's important to reflect on how best to **maximize your experience** while keeping the trip safe, enjoyable, and memorable. This section draws together the essential tips, practical resources, and inspiration for shaping itineraries that suit your pace, interests, and travel style.

Making the Most of Your Visit

The Yorkshire Dales offers a **blend of natural wonders, historic villages, cultural heritage, and outdoor adventures**. Whether your goal is to hike scenic trails, explore waterfalls, wander through charming villages, or relax in quaint tea rooms, a thoughtful approach to planning ensures you capture the region's essence without rushing.

- **Balance Adventure with Leisure:** Mix longer hikes and drives with slower, immersive experiences in towns, museums, and local eateries.
- **Embrace Flexibility:** Weather can change quickly; allow your itinerary to adapt so you can enjoy the best of the outdoors without stress.
- **Prioritize Highlights:** Focus on areas that match your interests—waterfalls, wildlife, historic sites, or cultural festivals—rather than attempting to see everything.

Suggested Approach to Itineraries

Your time in the Dales can vary from a short weekend to a full week. Here are some guiding principles for creating your own inspiring itineraries:

1. **Short Trips (2–3 Days):**

    - Concentrate on **southern and central Dales**: Skipton, Grassington, Malham, and Hawes.
    - Focus on a few key highlights, such as Malham Cove, Aysgarth Falls, and a market town experience.

2. **Medium Trips (4–5 Days):**

    - Explore both **southern and northern valleys**, including Swaledale and Wensleydale.
    - Include waterfalls, limestone formations, historic villages, and scenic drives like Buttertubs Pass.

3. **Extended Trips (7 Days or More):**

    - Take time to discover **hidden gems and remote areas**, including Arkengarthdale, Muker, Keld, and Nidderdale.
    - Incorporate **multi-day hikes**, historical sites, museum visits, local festivals, and farm-to-table food experiences.

Inspiring Itinerary Ideas

- **Nature & Photography Tour:** Focus on waterfalls, limestone pavements, viaducts, and valleys. Ideal for photographers and nature lovers.
- **Cultural & Heritage Trail:** Explore castles, abbeys, museums, and historic villages while tasting local cuisine.
- **Adventure & Activity Week:** Combine hiking, cycling, caving, and climbing with occasional village exploration.
- **Family-Friendly Journey:** Include gentle walks, creamery visits, local farms, and accessible villages for a relaxed pace.

Each itinerary can be customized according to **season, mobility, interests, and accommodation preferences**, giving travelers the freedom to create their ideal experience.

Practical Takeaways

- **Plan Ahead but Stay Flexible:** Book accommodations and key activities in advance, particularly in peak season.
- **Be Prepared for the Outdoors:** Always carry essentials, including waterproof clothing, sturdy footwear, maps, water, and snacks.
- **Use Local Knowledge:** Visitor centers, local guides, and residents can provide insider tips, hidden paths, and seasonal events.
- **Travel Responsibly:** Respect the environment, livestock, and local communities by following the Countryside Code.

Final Thoughts

The Yorkshire Dales is more than just a destination; it is an experience that combines **nature, history, culture, and adventure**. Whether wandering through a quiet village, hiking along a scenic ridge, or discovering a hidden waterfall, every moment is an opportunity to connect with the land and its heritage.

By combining **practical planning, safety awareness, and curiosity**, your journey through the Dales can become a **memorable and enriching adventure**. Use the suggested itineraries, maps, and tips in this guide as a foundation, but allow the **unexpected discoveries**—hidden lanes, local stories, and unplanned views—to make your trip uniquely yours.

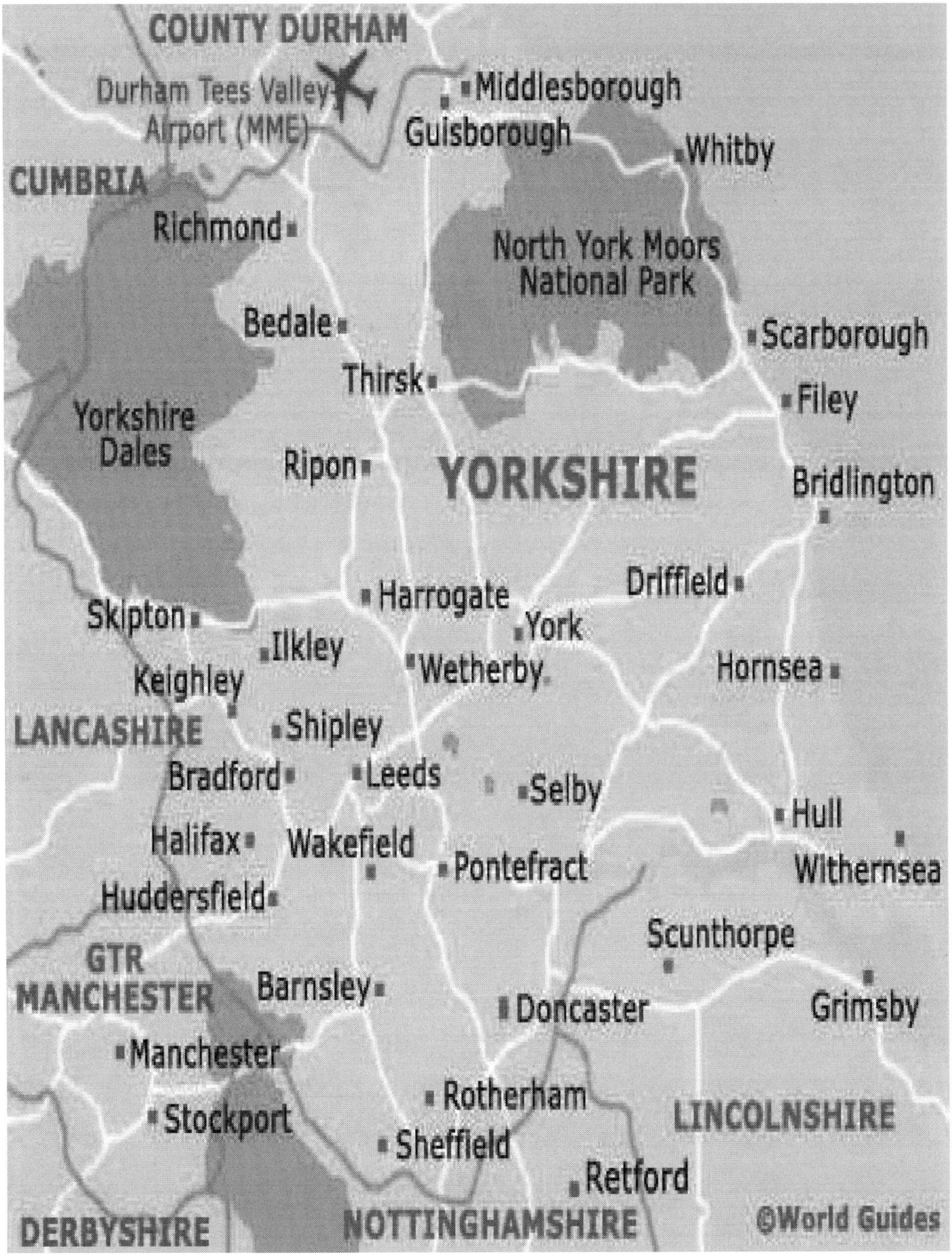
COUNTY DURHAM
Durham Tees Valley Airport (MME)
Middlesborough
Guisborough
Whitby
CUMBRIA
Richmond
North York Moors National Park
Bedale
Scarborough
Thirsk
Filey
Yorkshire Dales
Ripon
YORKSHIRE
Bridlington
Driffield
Harrogate
Skipton
York
Ilkley
Wetherby
Hornsea
Keighley
LANCASHIRE
Shipley
Bradford
Leeds
Selby
Hull
Halifax
Wakefield
Pontefract
Withernsea
Huddersfield
Scunthorpe
GTR MANCHESTER
Barnsley
Doncaster
Grimsby
Manchester
Rotherham
Stockport
LINCOLNSHIRE
Sheffield
Retford
DERBYSHIRE
NOTTINGHAMSHIRE
©World Guides

Printed in Dunstable, United Kingdom